READING THE BIBLE AS HISTORY

READING THE BIBLE AS HISTORY

Theodore Plantinga

G. R. WELCH COMPANY, LIMITED
Burlington **Ontario**

Scripture quotations are from The Revised Standard Version of The Holy Bible.

ISBN: 0-919532-58-6

© 1980 by G.R. Welch Company, Limited

G.R. Welch Company, Limited
960 Gateway
Burlington, Ontario
L7L 5K7 Canada

Dordt College Press
Sioux Center, Iowa
51250 U.S.A.

Printed in Canada

Contents

Let them thank the Lord for his steadfast love,
for his wonderful works to the sons of men!
Let them extol him in the congregation of the people,
and praise him in the assembly of the elders.
He turns rivers into a desert,
springs of water into thirsty ground,
a fruitful land into a salty waste,
because of the wickedness of its inhabitants.
He turns a desert into pools of water,
a parched land into springs of water.
And there he lets the hungry dwell,
and they establish a city to live in;
they sow fields, and plant vineyards,
and get a fruitful yield.
By his blessing they multiply greatly;
and he does not let their cattle decrease.
When they are diminished and brought low
through oppression, trouble, and sorrow,
he pours contempt upon princes
and makes them wander in trackless wastes;
but he raises up the needy out of affliction,
and makes their families like flocks.
The upright see it and are glad;
and all wickedness stops its mouth.
Whoever is wise, let him give heed to these things;
let men consider the steadfast love of the Lord.
(Psalm 107:31-43)

1

A History Book

The "battle for the Bible" did not begin in our time. For centuries questions have been raised about the Bible's trustworthiness and accuracy. So-called "higher critics" rejected the divine authority of Scripture and put the Bible on the same level as all other human books and writings.

Much of the debate as it continues in our time is a repetition of age-old charges and replies. If Christians sometimes tire of defending the Bible against its critics, it may well be because there seems to be nothing new under the sun when it comes to the long-standing dispute about the Bible's reliability.

One point often made in the debate is that the Bible should not be read as a science textbook. When Christians hear talk of discrepancies between the book of Genesis and the findings of modern science, they like to declare knowingly that the Bible is not a book of biology.

Now, there's nothing wrong with this response — on the surface, at least. There's no denying that the Bible was *not* written in biological language and does *not* rely on biological concepts. But could it be that an important insight is lost because of the widespread insistence and emphasis on this point?

There are also debates about the Bible's accuracy and reliability when it comes to its treatment of events of which we also have knowledge from other sources. When doubts about the biblical account of those events are raised, some Bible-believing Christians quickly interject: "But the Bible is not to be read as a history textbook either!" Other Christians aren't so sure.

Just what is a history textbook? Does "history" have its own special language and concepts that can be understood only by those who have studied the subject intensively? Some historians would undoubtedly like to view their discipline in such terms, but the fact is that historical scholarship has not developed in this direction.

Anyone who knows how to read can take "history books" out of the library and understand them — at some level of comprehension. This suggests that "history" is not as mysterious and esoteric as biology and the other natural sciences. There are major differences in language and approach between history and biology.

History can be written in naive, experiential, nonspecialized language that does not differ from the language you and I speak every day. The language of history is full of metaphors, analogies and figures of speech. Nations are personified; institutions take on a life of their own. But such metaphors and personifications are out of place in strictly scientific explanations. For a scientist, every concept must be justifiable in experiential and theoretical terms; personifications and loose analogies are simply ruled out.

Because the Bible does not speak the purified language of scientific concepts, we agree readily that it is not to be read as a biology book. But this well-founded belief does not in itself justify the conclusion that it is not a history book either. History is not so fussy about the language it uses.

The Bible, like many another book in which history is related, is written in nonspecialized, nonscientific language that does not differ greatly from the language used in history books even today. Therefore it seems that we do not have good grounds for arguing that the Bible is in no sense a history book. It is indeed a history book — and much more besides.

Why are so many Christians reluctant to affirm that the Bible is a history book? For one thing, some of the seemingly fantastic events recorded in Scripture offend us. We are ready for a God who deals with man in amazing, wondrous ways, but we balk at a God who knocks city walls flat, allows bears to maul children, and sends prophets into ecstatic trances for hours and days on end. Such stories are an affront to our common sense; they don't fit in with the preconceptions and preferences we bring to Bible reading. Hence we wonder whether there isn't some other way to read and interpret such stories. We try to explain them away or give them a "higher" meaning.

Such an approach to Scripture doesn't get a Christian very far. A Bible-believing Christian must be willing to let God's Word and Spirit dominate his understanding of the biblical message — and he must refrain from imposing his own conditions on the form in which the message comes to him. In orthodox circles, therefore, such a highhanded dismissal of parts of Scripture is rejected.

Yet, many of us have another serious complaint to make about the Bible's authors: they don't go about their work in as careful and methodical a manner as modern historians. They are careless about dates and details. They jump quickly from one event to another without letting us know what happened in between.

This complaint, too, can be handled without a great deal of difficulty. Nowhere do the Bible's authors claim to give a complete and comprehensive account of the events they describe. They are well aware that they are leaving out many details and episodes, and even refer us to other sources for further light on the subjects they touch on: *"Now the rest of his acts and all his ways, from first to last, behold, they are written in the Book of the Kings of Judah and Israel"* (II Chronicles 28:26). That may work for Ahaz, for we all have a copy of that "Book of the Kings," but what about Rehoboam? *"Now the acts of Rehoboam, from first to last, are they not written in the chronicles of Shemaiah the prophet and of Iddo the seer?"* (II Chronicles 12:15). Undoubtedly they are, but we don't happen to possess those chronicles written by Shemaiah and Iddo. Still, this doesn't make the account of Rehoboam's kingship any less true. Something short and incomplete can still be true — provided it's not misleading.

It is on such points that twentieth-century citizens of the Western world have a great deal of difficulty with the Bible. We are so deeply influenced by our science-saturated culture that we always want the details — the specifics — in quantitative terms, if possible. And that's just what the Bible's historical narratives fail to give us.

The point I wish to make at the outset, then, is that there are important differences between science and history. We are fully justified in claiming that the Bible is not a science textbook, for there can be no genuine science apart from the demand for specifics. When we read a scientific or scholarly account of an event, we demand details, specifics, concrete facts. And that's where the Bible does not seem to measure up. The Bible does not present us with science.

But does history bring with it the same demand for specifics? Different historians would answer this question in different ways. There are some who would love to turn history into a discipline as mysterious as chemistry; but most realize that history must speak the layman's language, much more so than chemistry or any other natural science. Written history arises out of group consciousness and national self-consciousness — in short, out of the awareness that any developing community has of its own past.

Now, if a community has an active grasp of its past — that is, an understanding of the past as something that remains alive, not just in archives but in the minds and hearts of the people — that past will be remembered and comprehended in its main lines only. No one could possibly remember all the details. But every patriotic citizen has some rough grasp of the main events in the birth and development of his own nation, enough to give him a perspective on his nation's history, and an outlook that will affect his view of the present and future. In other words, such remembered history, as it lives in the mind of the average man, is largely perspectival in character. It enables him to place himself, his family and his community in the larger stream of events called national history, and ultimately in the even larger context of world history.

A perspective on history may well be false and mistaken, of course, but the fact that it is a perspective does not automatically make it false — even though many perspectives on historical events are shot through with falsehood. This is an important point for any Christian understanding of history: historical truth is not just a matter of facts and details. Historical truth in the fuller sense, the kind of truth that makes history seem a living, interconnected whole, is impossible apart from a perspective.

A short account of a long series of historical events need not be any less true than a longer account of the same events. This is a point we should bear in mind especially when we consider the history of Jesus' life and work as related in Scripture. Many of us would like to have more detail; that's why so many spurious gospels were written to flesh out the picture of Jesus presented in the four gospels of the New Testament. But the four gospels are downright long-winded when compared to other historical accounts of Jesus presented in the Bible. Think of Peter's Pentecost sermon, for example:

> *Jesus of Nazareth, a man attested to you by God with mighty works and wonders and signs which God did through him in your midst, as you yourselves know — this Jesus, delivered up according to the definite plan and foreknowledge of God, you crucified and killed by the hands of lawless men. But God raised him up, having loosed the pangs of death, because it was not possible for him to be held by it* (Acts 2:22-4).

There you have the story of Jesus in a nutshell — all you really need to know. In the face of such a testimony, the feeble argument that Peter did not compose his account in the manner of a modern historian does not hold much water. Peter was speaking the truth!

The same applies to our own lives. When I fill out an application for a job, I may be asked for a brief biography — 200 words or less. There need be nothing untrue about the biography I write, although I may well feel a powerful urge to present myself in the best possible light — even to the point of misleading people.

Truth, therefore, is not to be confused with detail. We all know how details and statistics can be used in the service of the lie.

The Bible is — among other things — a history book. It gives us a more or less continuous account of the history of God's people up to and including the time of Christ and His disciples. Some episodes are described in considerable detail, and some are covered more than once. Certain periods are omitted for reasons not explained to us. All the same, what the Bible gives us is a running account of the history of the people called by God and chosen to be His special possession (Exodus 19:5).

The point we must bear in mind constantly is that biblical history was written for our instruction and edification — and not to satisfy our curiosity. That's why the perspectival element is uppermost in so many historical passages in the Bible. Events are described as part of the background, as the context within which we are to view the great saving acts of God. The history of God's people is presented as a way of showing who God is. That's why the numbers and details are often regarded as unimportant and are generally passed over lightly.

In addition to the continuous account of the history of God's people — and also at various points within that account — we find shorter passages that cover a great deal of history very quickly. We should learn to read such passages as clues to the meaning of the longer, more detailed narratives.

One such passage is Joshua 24:2-13. Before his death, the aged leader addresses God's people once again and begs them to commit themselves to the service of the Lord. He attaches a preface to his appeal in the form of a brief account of Israel's history. In this historical sketch he stresses that the Israelites received the land of Canaan as a gift from the hand of the Lord, who *"gave you a land on which you had not labored, and cities which you had not built, and you dwell therein; you eat the fruit of vineyards and oliveyards which you did not plant."* The details in this narrative are all intended to reinforce this point. The powerful truth of such a passage is to be sought not in its accuracy with regard to details but in the lesson — the challenge it presents.

Another such passage is Psalm 78, which seems to have been written around the time of David. The passage outlines Israel's unfaithfulness on the way to Canaan and her idolatry within the land of promise. But it ends on a note of grace:

He chose the tribe of Judah,
Mount Zion, which he loves. . . .
He chose David his servant,
and took him from the sheepfolds;
from tending the ewes that had young he brought him
to be the shepherd of Jacob his people,
of Israel his inheritance (Verses 68, 70-1).

What is the purpose of relating all that history? The Israelites were instructed to *"tell to the coming generation the glorious deeds of the Lord, and his might, and the wonders which he has wrought"* (Verse 4). Again, the point is not facts and details but a lesson for daily life, a revelation of Israel's covenant God.

Finally, I think of Stephen's speech just before he was stoned (Acts 7:2-53). Beginning with Abraham, Stephen briefly surveys the major episodes in Israel's history as the people of God. He speeds up when he gets to the period of the kings. You can almost feel the growing indignation of his hearers as he proceeds.

Stephen isn't allowed to bring his address to a stirring conclusion: he is dragged away and stoned when he claims to see the Son of man at the right hand of God. But he does utter a lament for his people: *"You stiff-necked people, uncircumcised in heart and ears, you always resist the Holy Spirit. As your fathers did, so do you. Which of the prophets did not your fathers persecute?"* (Verses 51-2). Stephen, too, relates history to make a point: the Jews *"received the law as delivered by angels and did not keep it"* (Verse 53).

To me the Bible is a history book full of lessons for us. The three historical passages mentioned above illustrate what all of biblical history is about. And the Bible *opens* with history in the form of the Torah, the teaching we need to guide us as we live in covenant with God.

The Bible is not a history textbook in any modern, twentieth-century sense, but our very salvation depends on the history it relates. That's why we must be thoroughly familiar with that history. Without such familiarity, the *non*historical passages will not reveal their full meaning to us either.

2

Redemptive History

Some Christians have no difficulty admitting that the Bible is a history book in some sense. They say, "Of course! The Bible presents us with *redemptive* history."

That's true, but it's not the whole story. When we maintain that the narratives found in the Bible represent a special brand of history (i.e., the history of our salvation), we are overlooking a few important points and reducing the scope of the Bible's message. We then run the risk of making man independent of God and picturing God simply as the one who restores the equilibrium when things go wrong on earth.

It is not enough to speak of "redemptive history" when the question of the Bible and history is raised. I shall present four reasons why such an approach to this question is too limited.

First of all, we forget that the Bible includes some historical narratives that fall outside the scope of redemptive history. Think of the opening verses of Genesis. They give us an account of the world's creation and man's fall into sin. Surely the fall is one of the most important historical — and historic — events recorded in Scripture. Yet, it falls outside the scope of redemptive history.

The fall is the *occasion* for redemptive history. That history begins when God comes to man after the fall with a promise — the famous promise that is often referred to as the "mother-promise" — *"I will put enmity between you* [the serpent] *and the woman, and between your seed and her seed; he shall bruise your head, and you shall bruise his heel"* (Genesis 3:15).

Secondly, we forget that some of the history recorded in Scripture has the character of general history that is not specifically tied in with God's plans for restoring and redeeming the fallen world. In fact, we sometimes wonder what it's doing in the Bible.

Early in Genesis, for example, we get a quick overview of cultural history before the flood — Jabal and Jubal and Tubal-cain. And toward the end we are offered a curious snippet of Egyptian political and economic history: we are told how Joseph, as "prime minister," furthered the financial interests of the Pharaoh at the expense of the people of Egypt (Genesis 47:13ff).

Thirdly, we must remember that biblical history is not all sweetness and light. What we read in the Bible is not just the history of salvation; it is also the history of judgment.

This makes perfectly good sense once we pause to think about it. God tells us that He is drawing a line through history and the creation, in preparation for the final separation. He will indeed redeem and renew His own, but those who resist Him will be banished and destroyed. That's why the prospect of God's "coming," the prospect of the "day of the Lord," gives rise to mixed feelings of hope and horror. *"Who can endure the day of his coming?"* Malachi rightly asked. *"And who can stand when he appears?"* (Malachi 3:2).

John the Baptist warned: *"His winnowing fork is in his hand, to clear his threshing floor, and to gather the wheat into his granary, but the chaff he will burn with unquenchable fire"* (Luke 3:17).

Amos advised the covenant people of his day not to be too eager for the coming of the day of the Lord: *"Woe to you who desire the day of the Lord! Why would you have the day of the Lord? It is darkness, and not light"* (Amos 5:18). The term *redemptive history* can mislead us, then, in that it tends to make us forget about judgment.

In the fourth place, we must be sure not to look upon the Bible as a comprehensive textbook recording *all* of redemptive history. There is much more to redemptive history than what is described in the Bible.

Abraham, for example, is certainly a key figure in redemptive history, but we are not told a great deal about him. Much more important than Abraham is Jesus Christ, whose life on earth is dealt with in four separate books of the Bible. All the same, there are many redemptive deeds that Jesus performed on earth as the promised Messiah of which Scripture tells us nothing. The apostle John testifies: *"But there are also many other things which Jesus did; were every one of them to be written, I suppose that the world itself could not contain the books that would be written"* (John 21:25).

All the same, "redemptive history" is a very useful concept when it comes to studying the Bible. Despite the reservations noted above, most of the narratives in Scripture can indeed be understood as episodes in God's dealings with man. We are shown how the Creator of the world struggles to put mankind back on the path to full communion with Him.

When we speak of the Bible as redemptive history, we soon find ourselves talking about "world history." We point out that only the redemption and healing wrought by Christ can turn the histories of the nations into a unified historical process moving toward the goal of cosmic redemption. If true harmony and peace are ever to reign on earth, if the historical fragmentation of the tower of Babel is ever to be reversed, it will only happen through the unification made possible by Christ's work of redemption and renewal.

The idea of world history — as opposed to the more limited idea of national and local history — requires thinking of all the strands as somehow coming together. It makes sense to speak of world history only if history is, or becomes, a unified process — a unity.

That unity embracing mankind as a whole is not something given at the outset of redemptive history. Rather, it is something to be *achieved.* And it will be achieved only through Christ, the Messiah. Therefore, we speak of Christ as the midpoint of world history and the focus of its meaning. The completion of His work of salvation and judgment will lead to His rule over the entire renewed earth. That's the goal of redemptive history — and therefore also of world history.

Such language is basically correct and helpful and scriptural provided we do not forget about the time *before* redemptive history. It was man's fall that made redemptive history necessary. God's Son, whom we speak of as the Christ, is not only the one who makes atonement for our sins; He is also the one through whom the world was made (John 1), the one who is *"before all things,"* the one in whom *"all things hold together"* (Colossians 1:17).

The purpose of the cosmic drama unfolded in Scripture is not man's restoration but God's glorification. Man is redeemed for the sake of God's glory and honor — and not because he possesses any intrinsic worthiness. This long-standing Calvinistic emphasis must also be allowed a role in shaping our understanding of biblical history as redemptive history.

The term *redemptive history* needs some clarification because of the inherent ambiguity of the word *history.* When we speak of history, we may be referring to either the events or the record of the events. Sometimes we aren't quite sure which one we mean. When I say that I'm interested in German history, I refer to both the events and the records of the events (i.e., documents and history books).

This distinction should be borne in mind when we approach Scripture with such a concept as redemptive history. In fact, it would be useful to carry the distinction a step further. When we speak of redemptive history, we could mean: a) the events in and through which God realizes His plan for mankind's salvation and judgment; b) the historical record of those events as seen from a human point of view, or c) the divine commentary on those events offered by writers who have received revelations from God.

First of all, redemptive history is a series of events. We think of how the Lord led His people out of Egypt, the mighty event or series of events to which so many later Scripture passages point when they speak of deliverance.

Secondly, it is a record of such events as seen from a human point of view. Take the book of Esther, for example. In that book we read about a threat to the survival of God's covenant people in the heart of the Persian empire. Mordecai suggests to Esther that the real purpose behind her elevation to the throne as Persia's queen may be to enable her to save her people in their hour of peril (Esther 4:14), but the writer of the book of Esther does not directly confirm this or even mention the name of God. He does not tell us of the Lord's intention in these events. He simply relates them from a human point of view. All the same, what he has written is a chapter of redemptive history containing a redemptive lesson for God's people.

Finally, redemptive history is reflection on the meaning of events; it is divine commentary. The writings of the prophets are full of interpretive statements that allow us to see how God views events in the lives of His people.

Think of Jehu, who was commissioned by the Lord through a prophet to dethrone King Jehoram and wipe out the house of Ahab (II Kings 9-10). Jehu even bragged about his *"zeal for the Lord"* in carrying out his assignment (10:16). But in the book of Hosea we find out that God did not see eye to eye with Jehu on how he carried out his mission: *"I will punish the house of Jehu for the blood of Jezreel"* (1:4). Apparently Jehu did the will of the Lord — but for his own selfish reasons, rather than out of any desire to obey the Lord.

We find a good deal of this type of commentary on events in the Bible, especially in the writings of the prophets. Hence it is futile to try to divide Old Testament writings into categories of "historical" and "prophetic." Many segments of the Old Testament contain both narrative and commentary in abundant measure.

3

Covenant History

If we are to bring the concept of redemptive history into proper focus, we must learn to view the events described in the Bible from the perspective of God's covenant with man. Because God offers us redemption *through* the covenant — remember that the promise of a Redeemer is also a covenant promise — the redemptive history recorded in the Old Testament does not deal indiscriminately with all the nations of the earth. On the contrary, it focuses on Israel and her relations with neighboring nations.

The reason for this is that God chose to approach mankind and work out His salvation through a particular people. During a period of great apostasy after the flood, the Lord called Abraham to leave his own land and people and gods — the "other gods" referred to by Joshua in his historical address to Israel at Shechem (Joshua 24) — and go to a land which the Lord would show him. Abraham responded in faith and God made a covenant with him.

The covenant was renewed repeatedly, and Abraham's descendants were included in it — but not all of them. Isaac was chosen and Ishmael rejected; Jacob was chosen and Esau rejected. Eventually the covenant circle grew and developed into a nation — Israel, named after its forefather Jacob. At Mount Sinai God took the entire nation into His covenant, and in the promised land the covenant with Israel was renewed again.

The terms of that covenant and the failure of the Israelites to live up to those terms are central to much of the history recorded in the Old Testament. Many centuries after Sinai, Daniel prays in Babylon for a restoration of Israel in her own land. He confesses that Israel has not kept the *covenant law* of Moses and has therefore been subjected to the *covenant judgment* Moses outlined when he gave the people the law: *"All Israel has transgressed thy law and turned aside, refusing to obey thy voice. And the curse and oath which are written in the law of Moses the servant of God have been poured out upon us, because we have sinned against him"* (Daniel 9:11).

Even though Israel has forfeited her covenant privileges through disobedience and unfaithfulness, Daniel continues to speak of "thy people," aware that God is faithful to His covenant promises and will not quickly let go of the people He has chosen as His special possession: *"O Lord, hear; O Lord, forgive; O Lord, give heed and act; delay not, for thy own sake, O my God, because* thy *city and* thy *people are called by thy name"* (Verse 19).

In the New Testament era, when the covenant is open to people of all tribes and nations, the status of its symbols and institutions is still an intense concern. When Jesus dies on the cross, the curtain of the temple is torn in two (Matthew 27:51; Mark 15:38). In the apostolic age there are lengthy debates about circumcision and the Old Testament ritual laws about purity. Slowly the meaning of Jeremiah's prophecy about a "new covenant" (Jeremiah 31:31-4) is understood and implemented. A *new* covenant! But God still deals with His people this way, and the completion of Christ's atoning work does not remove the need for a covenant between God and man.

In the preaching of the apostles, the covenant theme still looms large. Peter, in his Pentecost sermon, presents Jesus against the background of a covenant promise made to David: one of his descendants would be placed upon the throne (Acts 2:14ff). That promise, as Peter shows, has redemptive significance. When Paul preaches in Antioch of Pisidia, he also presents Jesus against the background of covenant history (Acts 13:16ff). Jesus is again identified as being of David's posterity.

When we look at the Bible as redemptive history, we cannot help but notice that not all of redemptive history is recorded there. Hence we wonder what principle of selection was used in the composition of the historical narratives. While we cannot give a full answer to this question, we can at least establish that *redemptive* history as recorded in Scripture follows *covenant* lines. God made His covenant with Abraham, Isaac, Jacob, and their sons after them, using the covenant line to bring the promised Messiah into the world.

If we keep these main lines before us, we will learn to avoid certain common mistakes in Bible reading. Because the Bible is such a massive book, we often wind up reading only a few favorite chapters or sentences. (Think of the short "texts" on which so many sermons are based.)

The Bible does not reveal its meaning to us if we limit our focus to short texts or sentences. In fact, the individual sentences that make up the Bible are often downright misleading when studied out of context.

We must not forget that many a passage in the Bible presents us with a record of what was said and done on a particular occasion. And much of what was said was falsehood. Hence there is false-hood recorded in the Bible. We cannot simply identify every statement in the biblical record as revealed truth.

In I Samuel 4:8 we read about *"the gods who smote the Egyptians with every sort of plague."* This statement is not accurate of course; it was *the Lord* — and no one else — who overthrew the might of the Egyptians. The statement is a quota-tion from the Philistines, who were frightened when they saw the Israelites approaching with the ark of the covenant. They gave expression to their fear in their own heathen terminology and concepts, which left no room for the God who created heaven and earth. No doubt what they said was recorded accurately by the author of the first book of Samuel, but the statement is false as it stands.

We find another example in II Samuel 7. David expresses a

desire to build a house for the Lord, and the prophet Nathan responds: *"Go, do all that is in your heart; for the Lord is with you"* (Verse 3). This time the statement comes from the Lord's prophet rather than a group of pagan soldiers. Hence we should be able to trust it as an indication of God's will. But when we read further, we discover that Nathan spoke too soon. The Lord does *not* want David to build Him a house — and He sends Nathan back to tell David not to do it. Again, the quotation is no doubt accurate, but the person making the statement was not speaking the truth, even if he believed he was. Nathan thought he knew the Lord's mind in this matter, but he was mistaken.

When we read the Bible as a record of redemptive history and covenant history, we must learn to pay special attention to the divine commentary. That's why the observations about Israel's history recorded in the books of the prophets are so instructive.

We should learn to be on the lookout for indications of how God viewed the events described in the Bible. Sometimes those indications are presented in indirect ways. The author of the book of Judges remarks repeatedly: *"In those days there was no king in Israel; every man did what was right in his own eyes."*

In some passages, larger segments of history are interpreted from a divine perspective. Consider this summary of the age of the judges:

Then the Lord raised up judges, who saved them out of the power of those who plundered them. And yet they did not listen to their judges; for they played the harlot after other gods and bowed down to them; they soon turned aside from the way in which their fathers had walked, who had obeyed the commandments of the Lord, and they did not do so. Whenever the Lord raised up judges for them, the Lord was with the judge, and he saved them from the hand of their enemies all the days of the judge; for the Lord was moved to pity by their groaning because of those who afflicted and oppressed them. But whenever the judge died, they turned back and behaved worse than their fathers, going after other gods, serving them and bowing down to them; they did not drop any of their practices or their stubborn ways (Judges 2:16-19).

This passage leads up to an explanation of an important factor in Israel's life as a nation: because of Israel's unfaithfulness, the Lord did not drive the other nations out of Canaan completely (Verse 23). Those nations remained there as a test, a perpetual problem for the Israelites, who were led into sin time and again when the Canaanites tempted them with their sensual idol worship.

The divine commentary in Scripture also opens our eyes to the interplay between the deeds and decisions of man and the initiatives taken by the Lord. When David sins by ordering a census, he is allowed to choose his punishment from three options. He chooses three days of pestilence. But as the pestilence approaches Jerusalem, David prays movingly:

> *Was it not I who gave command to number the people? It is I who have sinned and done very wickedly. But these sheep, what have they done? Let thy hand, I pray thee, O Lord my God, be against me and against my father's house; but let not the plague be upon thy people* (I Chronicles 21:17; Samuel 24:17).

The plague is halted, and David is commanded to build an altar. But earlier in the same passage we read: *"God sent the angel to Jerusalem to destroy it; but when he was about to destroy it, the Lord saw, and he repented of the evil"* (Verse 15). The Lord takes the initiative in halting the plague, but at the same time He is responding to David's prayer.

The divine commentary in Scripture is not always so clear and obvious. In the encounter between Moses and Pharaoh, we read repeatedly that Pharaoh hardened his heart or that his heart was hardened after the plague was lifted. But on some occasions we read that *the Lord* hardened Pharaoh's heart (Exodus 9:12; 10:20; 11:10). Later the Lord gave Moses a glimpse of the real issue in this struggle. He warned Moses that the Israelites had not yet seen the last of Pharaoh and the Egyptians: *"And I will harden Pharaoh's heart, and he will pursue them and I will get glory over Pharaoh and all his host; and the Egyptians shall know that I am the Lord"* (14:4).

The Bible is a book of history, then, a book recording the

history of salvation and judgment. The focus of the events it describes is the covenant relationship between God and His chosen people.

The key to the struggle is that God repeatedly takes the initiative for the sake of the glory of His name. Even man's redemption serves God's glory. That's the perspective we need if we are to comprehend the historical narratives in the Bible and find our own place in redemptive history.

4

Heaven and Earth

Who are the actors in the great drama of the history of salvation and judgment? God takes the initiative; He is the one who keeps events moving ahead to their climax and consummation. And we know that human beings — both believers and unbelievers — are also actors on the stage of history. Anyone else?

Scripture tells us that *"we are surrounded by so great a cloud of witnesses"* (Hebrews 12:1). We aren't always agreed on what to make of this text. Does it mean that the dead are watching our every move? Or does this text refer to the many created spirits that the Bible points to as agents in our history? The latter, it seems to me.

The Bible indicates clearly that spirits participate in human history, but it says nothing about the dead being involved in our lives — with the possible exception of the mysterious case of the "spirit" that appeared when Saul paid a visit to the witch of Endor (I Samuel 28). And in that story it is far from obvious that the figure that appeared to the witch was really the spirit of Samuel.

Who, or what, are those nonhuman spirits? The Bible calls them *angels* and tells us that they are *"ministering spirits sent forth to serve"* (Hebrews 1:14). But some of those spirits, who, like us, are beings created by God, rebelled against their Maker and now do everything in their power to oppose Him. Those fallen angels or demons, with Satan as their head, play an important role in the struggle here on earth.

Now, many Christians have a hard time comprehending talk about "spirits" and therefore resist believing in the world of spirits. The Bible's stories about angels and demons sound too much like primitive folklore to be accepted by "modern man." In biblical times there were also doubters, despite all the appearances of angels and demons. The Sadducees, we are told, claimed *"that there is no resurrection, nor angel, nor spirit"* (Acts 23:8).

Some Christian theologians have argued that appearances of angels are ultimately to be regarded as appearances of God Himself. Spinoza and Schleiermacher, both advocates of a "higher" monotheism that turns into pantheism, maintained that Jesus Himself did not believe in angels and that He only put up with talk of angels in order to bring His message in language that the people of His time would understand. I suspect that these two mystics have a lot of sympathizers even in orthodox Christian circles. Angels and demons just don't fit into our carefully defined ontology, our modern conception of reality.

Many of us, then, are reluctant to think in terms of angels involved in human history as servants of God or agents of the evil one. And we feel a similar reluctance about God's own involvement. We are inclined to make God keep His distance, allowing Him to intervene only occasionally in human history. We are attracted by the old idea of God as the "clockmaker" who fashions the world, gets it running, and then leaves it alone except for an occasional adjustment. Such a view of God leaves us free to believe that it is *man* who makes history.

In some Christian circles, such thinking has reached a highly developed stage. In fact, one could speak of a theology of heaven and earth. This theology, carefully defined, is bound up with Greek ideas concerning time and eternity. The world is in time; God is eternal. Therefore, direct contact between God and the world is sporadic at best. God can enter history through a special event like the incarnation, but apart from such exceptions, there is no room for Him in our world.

And what about heaven? Since heaven is part of the realm of eternity, there is an unbridgeable gulf between heaven and earth; they are entirely separate dimensions of reality. As believers die, they slip off one by one to the realm of eternity. At the end of time, all believers will be united in the eternal realm known as heaven, where God is. There they will dwell forever.

This theological tradition keeps God in His heaven and leaves the earth for man. As for angels and demons, they don't quite fit in. If there are angels, they must be outside time, in heaven. But then they can't very well move back and forth between heaven and earth, for there is a great chasm between earth and heaven.

This thinking, which has become all too familiar in orthodox Protestant circles, does not reflect the language of the Bible. What comes through strongly in the Bible is the idea of the unity of heaven and earth, a unity that was shattered by sin but is destined to be restored.

Before sin rendered the world unfit to be God's dwelling place, God was not confined to an eternal realm called heaven. The creation story emphasizes God's preoccupation with the earth, His delight in what He made. Just before the encounter between God and man occasioned by the original sin, we read that Adam and Eve *"heard the sound of the Lord God walking in the garden in the cool of the day"* (Genesis 3:8). And why not? *"In the beginning God created the heavens and the earth"* (Genesis 1:1).

At the end of the period in which we now live, heaven and earth will undergo a complete transformation and renewal. John reports in his account of his visions: *"I saw a new heaven and a new earth; for the first heaven and the first earth had passed away"* (Revelation 21:1). The heaven of which the Bible speaks, then, is a created domain; it is not an eternal realm that is as far removed as possible from the earth, and is much holier than the earth could ever be.

That heaven and earth are in frequent contact and are ultimately to be viewed as one cosmic arena is suggested in numerous Bible passages. The apostle John, from his earthly perspective, sees heaven opened (Revelation 19:11). It is also opened when Jesus is baptized: *"Immediately he saw the heavens opened and the Spirit descending upon him like a dove, and a voice came from heaven . . ."* (Mark 1:10; Matthew 3:16; Luke 3:22). This event is not to be interpreted as a vision on Jesus' part. John the Baptist declares: *"I saw the Spirit descend as a dove from heaven, and it remained on him"* (John 1:32).

The apostle John reports that he actually looked into heaven and saw an open door (Revelation 4:1). He saw portents in heaven (12:1; 15:1) and angels coming down from heaven (10:1; 18:1). Coming down to where? The earth, of course. The events and struggles in heaven are decisive for the fate of those who are on the earth.

The two ascensions described in Scripture also testify to the close ties between heaven and earth, but the story of Christ's ascension as recorded by Luke in Acts does not mention heaven. We read that *"a cloud took him out of their sight"* (Acts 1:9). Then the two messengers in white robes testify: *"This Jesus, who was taken up from you into heaven, will come in the same way as you saw him go into heaven"* (Verse 11). The account of the ascension that Luke gives at the end of his gospel also mentions heaven as Jesus' destination, and the disputed ending of Mark's gospel does so as well. Finally, when Elijah was swept up before Elisha's eyes (the other ascension in Scripture), we read that he *"went up by a whirlwind into heaven"* (II Kings 2:11).

There is also movement from heaven to earth. The manna provided for the Israelites in the wilderness, which is an apt symbol of the grace of God, is characterized as *"bread from heaven"* (John 6:31).

But what comes from heaven isn't all blessing! When the time arrives to destroy Sodom and Gomorrah, fire falls from heaven (Genesis 19:24). Fire from heaven might conceivably be understood as fire from the sky, such as lightning, for the terms "heaven" and "the heavens" are often used in the Bible to refer to the sky. But the writer of Genesis is specific: he speaks of *"brimstone and fire* from the Lord *out of heaven."*

Fire from heaven also strikes the soldiers of King Ahaziah when they approach Elijah to arrest him (II Kings 1). Two companies of soldiers are described as being consumed by fire *"from heaven,"* the same kind of *"fire of the Lord"* that lit Elijah's drenched offering on Mount Carmel in the contest with the priests of Baal (I Kings 18).

It is clear, then, that the Bible speaks of a good deal of commerce and movement between heaven and earth. But it does not explain — to a philosopher's satisfaction — what relationship there is between heaven and earth in the period between the fall and the final restoration.

Heaven is not a place to which we can travel of our own volition. In principle it is possible for man to travel to the planets and the stars, but a spaceship will not enable man to enter heaven. Then what, or where, is heaven?

The problematic relationship between heaven and earth cannot be explained in scientific terms. Yet, it seems to me that the question of the relationship can indeed be answered on a different level — the level of the Bible's own language.

Once man and the world were plunged into sin, the Lord God could no longer walk in the garden. He had to withdraw from the world He had made. But He decided to redeem that world and again make it a suitable habitation for Himself. One day He would live in the hearts of men. In time, the whole earth would be filled with the knowledge of His glory (Habakkuk 2:14), with the radiance of His presence. But in the meantime God would limit His special nearness to heaven, which was apparently not corrupted by man's fall into sin.

Since heaven is still filled with God's glory and presence, its brilliance is too much for the fallen earth to bear. This we see reflected in Scripture. The earth is given a taste of heaven on the Mount of Transfiguration. Jesus takes on dazzling glory: *"He was transfigured before them, and his garments became glistening, intensely white, as no fuller on earth could bleach them"* (Mark 9:2-3). Peter, James and John are not comfortable in this environment. Despite their close ties with Jesus, the impurity of sin and this fallen world clings to them. Peter makes an inappropriate suggestion to the effect that Jesus take up residence in this special place. Mark reports that Peter *"did not know what to say, for they were exceedingly afraid"* (Verse 6). There must be some distance between heaven and earth, Peter sensed.

This is likewise reflected in the stories about Moses and his encounters with God. We read that the Lord *"used to speak to Moses face to face, as a man speaks to his friend"* (Exodus 33:11). We don't know quite what to make of such a text, but it does at least indicate that Moses was in God's presence in some special way. The glory that rubbed off on him was too much for the Israelites to bear. Moses had to wear a veil over his face. Earth cannot abide the nearness of heaven (34:29ff).

Heaven withdraws from the earth as a result of sin, but it does *disclose* itself on certain occasions. The people on the earth are not free to get a glimpse of heaven whenever they wish. Heaven *reveals* itself — and then only to those who have eyes to see.

Think of the well-known story of Balaam and his donkey. The angel messenger confronts Balaam, but Balaam does not have eyes to see him (Numbers 22). The donkey however, sees the angel, and finally has to speak up to bring Balaam around. The angel chose to reveal himself first to the donkey and then to Balaam.

Another revelation from heaven recorded in Scripture is selective in the same way. When Jesus stopped Paul on the road to Damascus, He revealed Himself only to Paul, even though the people traveling with him apparently saw or heard something as well (see Acts 9 and 22). It is heaven that takes the initiative in disclosing itself to the earth.

Stephen, too, is allowed a vision of heaven opening: he sees *"the Son of man standing at the right hand of God"* (Acts 7:55-6), but the vision is not shared by his accusers.

What we can say on solid biblical grounds, then, is that forces and agents from heaven can reveal themselves to those who are on the earth and that they participate in earthly history. This applies to demons as well as angels. The "cloud of witnesses" all around us enjoys the privilege of retaining its incognito. Satan and his hosts can go about their work without revealing themselves to us, unless it suits their purposes.

Heaven, God and the created spirits play a role in the history of man, which has become the history of salvation and judgment. The Bible provides some intriguing examples showing us just how much events in heaven affect what goes on here on earth.

Think of the puzzling scenes recorded in the first two chapters of the book of Job. Those who are wedded to the idea of an eternal, serene, unchanging, heavenly realm above the vicissitudes of time should read through these chapters carefully, for they show us a lively argument between God and His great adversary Satan. The accuser scoffs at the idea that Job's love for God is pure and unselfish. God accepts the challenge and allows Satan to plague Job.

If ever we needed biblical evidence that events on the earth are shaped by events in heaven, the book of Job provides it. That's one of the reasons why it's in the Bible. Poor Job is struck by one calamity after another. Satan torments him — with God's permission!

In many instances recorded in Scripture, God sends angels to assist His people. But He also works through "evil" spirits, that is, spirits that act as agents of His judgment. After Saul is rejected as Israel's king, he goes through a great deal of mental anguish and torment. Eventually he throws his spear at David. Why? We read that an *"evil spirit from the Lord came upon Saul"* (I Samuel 19:9).

An even more striking example is to be found in a chilling episode that is not as well known as the story of Saul's attempt on David's life. Ahab, a godless king of Israel, proposes to go to war against the Syrians. He prevails upon King Jehoshaphat of Judah to join him, but Jehoshaphat wants to consult a prophet of the Lord. Ahab summons four hundred prophets, and they all tell him what he wants to hear: victory is assured. Jehoshaphat is still dubious and asks for a real prophet. Isn't there a true prophet around somewhere? Ahab reluctantly summons Micaiah, who first mocks the four hundred false prophets by repeating their prophecy. When he finally passes on what the Lord has revealed to him, he tells the two kings that he sees *"all Israel scattered upon the mountains, as sheep that have no shepherd"* (I Kings 22:17). He then goes on to give us a glimpse of what happens behind the scenes, in heaven:

I saw the Lord sitting on his throne, and all the host of heaven standing beside him on his right hand and on his left; and the Lord said, "Who will entice Ahab, that he may go up and fall at Ramoth-gilead?" And one said one thing, and another said another. Then a spirit came forward and stood before the Lord, saying, "I will entice him." And the Lord said to him, "By what means?" And he said, "I will go forth, and will be a lying spirit in the mouth of all his prophets." And he said, "You are to entice him, and you shall succeed; go forth and do so" (Verses 19-22).

Ahab's fate is sealed, and he dies in battle.

There is interchange between heaven and earth that proves decisive for the history of salvation and judgment. But it is only through revelation that we learn a little of what goes on in heaven.

The book of Daniel shows us how much there is to this heavenly background that remains out of sight. The aged prophet prays for Jerusalem's restoration, but for a long time he receives no answer to his prayer. Finally, a heavenly messenger appears before him with an explanation:

Fear not, Daniel, for from the first day that you set your mind to understand and humbled yourself before your God, your words have been heard, and I have come because of your words. The prince of the kingdom of Persia withstood me twenty-one days; but Michael, one of the chief princes, came to help me, so I left him there with the prince of the kingdom of Persia and came to make you understand what is to befall your people in the latter days (Daniel 10:12-14).

The book of Revelation also indicates clearly that there is a cosmic struggle going on, a struggle that involves both heaven and earth. Hence it is a fitting conclusion to the Bible, for it emphasizes that heaven and earth are ultimately meant to be joined; that they belong together. *"Behold, I make all things new"* (Revelation 21:5).

We are getting closer and closer to the time when the Lord God will again be able to walk in the garden in the cool of the day, when the Immanuel promise ("God with us") will be completely fulfilled, when God will live in unbroken communion with His people and His creation. That's the goal of history. But without the Bible's divine commentary on earthly events, we would have no way of knowing the final destination.

5

Culture and Calling

Liberal Protestantism has its own way of reading the Bible — a way that makes an effort to take history into account. The religion presented in the Bible took centuries to develop, we are told. It finally reached its culmination in Jesus, who is the greatest religious and moral leader of all time. The life of Jesus presents us with a vivid example of unselfish serenity in all of life's situations — a serenity that could be ours as well.

This magnanimous approach to Scripture even has some words of praise for the Old Testament. Many of the episodes related there may make us raise our eyebrows or even throw up our hands in horror, but the Mosaic legislation does contain some very advanced ideas for its time. Those surprisingly progressive notions of social justice bore fruit in Israel's life as a nation. We think of a man like Boaz, who knew that his personal prosperity brought with it certain obligations toward the poor. Israel ranks right next to Greece as an advanced country providing ideas and ideals on which Western civilization is based.

This outlook on ancient Israel and the Old Testament emphasizes history in that it stresses that higher ethical and religious ideas (for example, monotheism) emerged slowly with the passage of time. But it does not make much of Israel's fate as a nation, for the glorious kingdom of Boaz, David and Solomon eventually disintegrated and collapsed. The ideals of ancient Israel live on not in a political or social order but in the ethical teachings of Jesus.

This reading of the Bible, which is gaining ground in orthodox circles too, may have a certain appeal for the heirs of the Humanist tradition, but it does not reflect the Bible's own emphases.

The Old Testament was written by Jews, but it was not intended to glorify Israel as a nation. David, Israel's greatest king, is depicted as an adulterer and a murderer and a weak father. Solomon, his fabled successor, is described as a husband who could not say no to his wives. Jacob, the forefather who gave his name to the nation, is introduced as a scheming deceiver. And Moses, the leader who presided over the birth of Israel as a nation, is portrayed as a frightened man who used every device he could think of in an effort to escape the task to which God called him.

The emphasis in Israel's history as written by the Jews themselves does not fall on the heroics of that nation's leaders. We are all familiar with self-serving memoirs of political leaders, but the only book in the Bible reminiscent of memoirs written by someone out to present himself in the best possible light is Daniel. The Bible is not reticent when it comes to the sins and shortcomings of the saints.

When the Bible sketches the development of the chosen people toward redemption through the Messiah, it makes no effort to hide all the failures, false starts, mistakes, and discontinuity. The Bible emphasizes the initiatives that *God* takes, repeatedly, to keep the process moving ahead. Left to itself, the historical process would never lead to a Redeemer. This must be borne in mind when we consider the question of culture and calling.

The term *culture* is familiar to Bible readers because of the "cultural mandate," the commission given to man at the beginning of history (before the fall) and repeated after the flood. When man was created, God said to him: *"Be fruitful and multiply, and fill the earth and subdue it; and have dominion over the fish of the sea and over the birds of the air and over every living thing that moves upon the earth"* (Genesis 1:28). The command to be fruitful and multiply and fill the earth also came to Noah and his family, together with more instructions (Genesis 9).

This cultural mandate should be viewed as pointing implicitly to the process called history. And man's history, if it unfolds in accordance with the will of God as expressed in the cultural mandate and in the many laws given to man, should lead to blessing for the entire earth. Obedience, we are told, normally results in blessing.

But that's not how history has developed. Just as God was greatly displeased with what He saw on earth before the flood, He was repeatedly outraged after the flood by the sins of men, including the people who had received His special favor. The famous tower of Babel incident already illustrates how much mankind was out of step with God's purposes.

This disharmony between God's purposes and man's desires as reflected in the historical unfolding of human culture is the background to the many stories about "calling" in the Bible. The failure of the normal route of human culture made God's special calling necessary.

The development of culture in accordance with God's revealed will was not abandoned by God as a means of blessing. Think of the rise of a Mediterranean Greco-Roman civilization as a preparation for the spreading of the gospel, and also of the invention of the printing press just before the Reformation. Yet, special callings became necessary, over and over again, to accomplish God's goal. And those callings often came to people who were not thinking in terms of serving as God's agents in history.

Many of the most dramatic callings recorded in the Bible came at times when there seemed to be no progress in redemptive history. When I speak here of "progress," I am referring to the promised battle between the seed of the woman and the seed of the serpent. In the garden of Eden the serpent had won the first round. Now the seed of the woman (God's chosen people) would have to develop to a point where it would be capable of dealing the serpent a fatal blow. Ultimately that blow would be struck by the Redeemer to be born of God's people. But the meaning of the promise about the Redeemer only became clear in the course of redemptive history; at the very outset man was given no more than a vague promise of victory.

In the time of Noah, redemptive history was not making much progress. *"Now the earth was corrupt in God's sight, and the earth was filled with violence. And God saw the earth, and behold, it was corrupt; for all flesh had corrupted their way upon the earth"* (Genesis 6:11-12). It was in this situation that God announced to Noah that He meant to destroy the earth. But with this announcement came a special calling: Noah was to build a huge ark to protect a few people and animals from death in the raging waters of the flood.

We should note that in this case, as in so many others, the calling is not to be identified with conversion. Even before Noah was called to build the ark, he was a *"righteous man, blameless in his generation"* (Genesis 6:9).

This is not to say that a call to faith is never coupled with a call to a specific task to be performed on the Lord's behalf. Still, most of the people in the Bible who were called to carry out special assignments were already believers.

Paul might be cited as an example to the contrary, but I would then ask whether his dramatic encounter with Christ on the road to Damascus was really a conversion in the strict sense. Wasn't Paul raised as a believer? He testified that he served God with a clear conscience just as his fathers had (II Timothy 1:3).

Paul, living in the special period between Jesus' ascension and the day when the Lord finally closed the door on the Jews as His covenant people, sinned greatly by failing to acknowledge that Jesus of Nazareth was indeed the Christ. But when Jesus personally confronted Paul, Paul fell to his knees. Immediately he was sent on to Damascus to prepare for his mission as an apostle — redirected and put to work. (We are reminded of another stubborn believer, Jonah, who was redirected in a more literal sense and made to carry out the calling God had in mind for him.)

Paul himself describes the Damascus road experience in terms of calling in the Letter to the Galatians. He tells us that he was taught the gospel through a *"revelation of Jesus Christ"* (1:12).

What was the purpose of that revelation? Was it a call to faith, or a call to take up a special task? *"He who had set me apart before I was born, and had called me through his grace, was pleased to reveal his Son to me, in order that I might preach him among the Gentiles"* (Verses 15-16).

God also took the initiative to move redemptive history ahead when He called Abraham to separate himself from his own land and people (Genesis 12). Bear in mind that Abraham's family served "other gods" beyond the river (Joshua 24:2). God decided that it was necessary to separate a family and a people for His service. That could only be done by beginning with an actual physical separation and a cultural and social isolation; hence the nomadic life in tents.

Even so, the chosen family continued to cling to "other gods." Rachel, the wife of Abraham's grandson Jacob, took idols with her when she set out for Canaan with her husband. The presence of those idols contributed to the sin and heartaches in Jacob's household. His daughter was raped, and his sons misused the sacred covenant sign of circumcision as they murdered the men of Shechem in retaliation. When this impasse in redemptive history was reached and the chosen people were in deep danger of full apostasy, God again took the initiative by calling someone: He reminded Jacob of his vow to return to Bethel and told him that it was time to fulfill that vow. But purification was necessary first. The household had to be cleansed of those "other gods." Rachel's idols were finally buried under a tree (Genesis 35).

Hundreds of years later, in the time of Moses, God's chosen people were again at a low ebb. They worked as slaves of the Egyptians, and their faith had dwindled to a dangerous low point. God once more took the initiative by calling a leader — Moses, who came upon the burning bush. The Lord had to do a lot of talking to get Moses to accept the assignment. Even then this former Egyptian prince, who was appointed by God to be the leader and deliverer of His people, was lax in his devotion to God's covenant: he did not bother to have his own son circumcised (Exodus 4:24-6).

Moses, then, was hardly a leader who rose from the ranks of the people. Instead he was given to the people by God after an

extensive period of preparation that included a first-rate educa-
tion at Pharaoh's court and forty nomadic years in the wilderness.

The time of the Judges was another low point in Israel's history.
God's people were living in the promised land, but they had not
taken possession of it as the rightful owners. Marauding
Midianites were so completely in control that the Israelites went
about much of their work in secret, for fear that the Midianites
would take their produce from them.

In this deplorable situation, the Lord again took the initiative.
The angel of the Lord appeared to Gideon, a frightened Israelite
going about his work in secret, and greeted him in seemingly
sarcastic language: *"The Lord is with you, you mighty man of
valor"* (Judges 6:12). Gideon was a long way from being a man of
valor, but with the Lord's help he managed to become one. In a
campaign that opened with an audacious night attack, he
delivered the Israelites from Midianite oppression.

In the time of Ahab and Jezebel, things again looked dark for
God's people — at least, for those who lived in the northern
kingdom of the ten tribes. The king and his foreign queen openly
promoted idolatry and allowed the name of the Lord to be
scorned. The land suffered greatly as a result. Finally the Lord
took the initiative once more by calling someone to a special task.
He sent a prophet to an army officer named Jehu with a command
and a promise:

> *Thus says the Lord the God of Israel, I anoint you king over the
> people of the Lord, over Israel. And you shall strike down the
> house of Ahab your master, that I may avenge on Jezebel the
> blood of my servants the prophets, and the blood of all the
> servants of the Lord. For the whole house of Ahab shall perish;
> and I will cut off from Ahab every male, bond or free, in Israel.
> And I will make the house of Ahab like the house of Jeroboam
> the son of Nebat, and like the house of Baasha the son of
> Ahijah. And the dogs shall eat Jezebel in the territory of
> Jezreel, and none shall bury her* (II Kings 9:6-10).

Now, it is not the case that God must take the initiative and call
some surprised or reluctant individual *each time* things go awry.

Sometimes a leader steps forward of his own volition. Think of Nehemiah, the cupbearer at the court of King Artaxerxes. Nehemiah heard that little progress was being made in the restoration of Jerusalem. This upset him greatly, and he prayed to the Lord to be allowed to play a leading role in Jerusalem's restoration. Then he spoke to the king about this matter, and his request was granted (Nehemiah 1-2).

In some cases, God calls someone to a special task not so much to change the course of events as to drive a certain point home to the covenant people. The prophets Jeremiah and Ezekiel were often called on to do strange things in an effort to get the message across to people in a way they would understand. The prophet Hosea may have received the strangest calling of all: *"Go, take to yourself a wife of harlotry and have children of harlotry, for the land commits great harlotry by forsaking the Lord"* (Hosea 1:2). This may seem an extreme way of making a point, but Israel's situation was extreme.

Sometimes God's calling clearly overrides the provisions of His law. We find no clearer example than the special call that came to Abraham one day: *"Take your son, your only son Isaac, whom you love, and go to the land of Moriah, and offer him there as a burnt offering upon one of the mountains"* (Genesis 22:2). The Bible strongly condemns taking human life as a sacrifice. All the same, that was the command Abraham received. And he went far enough in carrying out the command to make it clear that he was willing to do what was asked of him. For this he received God's praise.

In other instances God called individuals or Israel as a nation to wipe out a family or an entire nation (for example, the peoples in Canaan). The God who discourages violence and declares that vengeance belongs to Him (Deuteronomy 32:35, Psalm 94:1; Romans 12:19) sometimes asks human beings to exercise that vengeance on His behalf. Again, the calling supersedes the law. God is not bound by His own law in what He can tell people to do.

The many stories in which God calls people to a special task are well known to us. (Think of the calling of the disciples of Jesus.) The point that needs to be made here is simply that man's role on earth is not exhausted in the cultural mandate and in obedience to the general directives of God's law. We must learn to see man as an agent in the history of salvation and judgment as it unfolds under God's guidance. God is leading that history toward its preordained goal. As we read the redemptive history recorded in Scripture, we must keep our eyes open to see how God repeatedly takes the initiative in coming to man with a specific calling.

6

Freedom in History

God has laid down certain general guidelines for the unfolding of human life and history. We often sum up those guidelines by speaking of "the law." People who live by "the law" may rightly expect God's blessing on their lives.

But "the law" alone will never lead human history to its redemptive goal. That's why God sometimes intervenes by coming to some human being with a special calling to a particular task or assignment. In these situations God takes the historical initiative, just as He takes the initiative in seeking us out individually and inviting us to enter His Kingdom.

A view of history that emphasizes only God's initiatives, however, would not do justice to history as presented in Scripture. There are many passages in the Bible that give us a glimpse of *God's* involvement in human affairs, but the bulk of the historical narrative still concerns the deeds of *men*.

History is not just a story of specific callings and divine initiatives aimed at clearly defined ends. Biblical history is also the story of man's varied *responses* to God's revelation. And in those responses man is free to some extent.

The notion of man's freedom in history may pose theological

problems for some. But it is not my purpose to explore the tangled set of issues involved in the doctrine of predestination. Instead, I propose to draw attention to Scripture's own language about history. In what sense does Scripture depict man as free?

No abstract theological definitions and distinctions are needed at this point, for it seems to me that the key to understanding the freedom allotted to man and to a creation groaning under the consequences of sin is *distance.*

As we noted earlier, the opening chapters of the Bible presuppose close ties between heaven and earth: the Lord God walks in the garden in the cool of the day (Genesis 3:8). But the frightful, ugly presence of sin drives God some distance away; His special presence no longer fills the earth. Scripture depicts God as maintaining an intense interest in the events on earth, while at the same time usually allowing those events to take their own course.

That there is distance between God and human history comes through especially at the beginning of biblical history, before the formation of the covenant community. In the time of Noah, the Lord seemed to be watching from a distance: *"The Lord saw that the wickedness of man was great in the earth, and that every imagination of the thoughts of his heart was only evil continually. And the Lord was sorry that he had made man on the earth, and it grieved him to his heart"* (Genesis 6:5-6). The Lord then came a little closer; intervening with the flood. But after the flood the distance was still there, despite the covenant with Noah.

In time mankind undertook a great building project to glorify the name of man — the tower of Babel. Again the Lord seemed to be watching from a distance. Finally we are told: *"And the Lord came down to see the city and the tower, which the sons of men had built"* (Genesis 11:5).

Later in history, when the wickedness of Sodom and Gomorrah became too much for heaven to bear, the Lord came down again. He visited Abraham and told him: *"Because the outcry against Sodom and Gomorrah is great and their sin is very grave, I will go down to see whether they have done altogether according to the outcry which has come to me"* (Genesis 18:20-1).

We get the same sense of distance between God and the peoples of the earth in Psalm 2:

Why do the nations conspire,
and the peoples plot in vain?
The kings of the earth set themselves,
and the rulers take counsel together,
against the Lord and his anointed (Verses 1-2).

What is the Lord's response? *"He who sits in the heavens laughs; the Lord has them in derision"* (Verse 4). Yet He keeps His distance, until He can stand it no longer. The psalmist counsels:

Now therefore, O kings, be wise;
be warned, O rulers of the earth.
Serve the Lord with fear,
with trembling kiss his feet,
lest he be angry, and you perish in the way;
for his wrath is quickly kindled (Verses 10-11).

Paul, too, gives us an indication that God adopts a "hands off" policy toward the nations in the early stages of redemptive history. Preaching in Lystra, he explains that God *"allowed all the nations to walk in their own ways"* in *"past generations"* (Acts 14:16).

Much of the distance between God and human history is overcome in the covenant. God again wishes to dwell in the midst of His people on the earth, so that the Immanuel promise ("God with us") may be fulfilled. The symbols of the covenant (for example, the ark of the covenant, the tabernacle, the temple) give Him a foothold on the earth as it is being reclaimed and renewed.

The purpose of covenant worship and service, then, is to make God come nearer, to make Him come down from heaven and bring His presence closer. Hence Isaiah's prayer: *"O that thou wouldst rend the heavens and come down . . . to make thy name known to thy adversaries, and that the nations might tremble at thy presence!"* (Isaiah 64:1-2).

God's presence — His coming down — involves great risks. This the people of Israel found out after they entered the covenant with the Lord at Mount Sinai. The mountain quaked when the

Lord descended (Exodus 19:18-20). But the people did not learn a lesson from this fearsome sight, for they fell into the sin of worshiping the golden calf while Moses was on the mountain. That sin nearly led to a complete rupture of the newly established covenant intimacy. The Lord proposed to reestablish the distance: *"Now therefore let me alone,"* He said to Moses, *"that my wrath may burn hot against them and I may consume them; but out of you I will make a great nation"* (Exodus 32:10). Moses interceded for the people, and *"the Lord repented of the evil which he thought to do to his people"* (Verse 14). Yet He told Moses that it would be better if He were not with or "among" His people: *"I will not go up among you, lest I consume you in the way"* (33:3ff). He would send His angel to go with them instead. But Moses pleaded successfully to have this decision reversed as well.

By keeping His distance, then, the Lord provides a measure of freedom for those involved in human history. This is also apparent from what the Bible says about the demons, the servants of Satan, who play an important role in the events on earth.

The demons are free to go about their destructive work for a time, as we see from an encounter between Jesus and some demons who cried out to Him: *"What have you to do with us, O Son of God? Have you come here to torment us before the time?"* (Matthew 8:29). Those demons enjoyed a measure of freedom, not because they had the power to resist God's will, but because God *allowed* them their freedom.

Yet the freedom of the demons has definite limits, as we see from Job's story. Satan himself appears before God to scoff at Job's devotion. Twice he asks permission to put Job to the test, and twice permission is granted — but each time within certain limits.

Limits on Satan are also referred to in John's vision recorded in Revelation 20: *"Then I saw an angel coming down from heaven, holding in his hand the key of the bottomless pit and a great chain. And he seized the dragon, that ancient serpent, who is the Devil and Satan, and bound him for a thousand years"* (Verses 1-2). Thus the demons are not completely free, even though they do enjoy an undeniable measure of freedom.

Human beings who reject God also enjoy some freedom. As we have seen (p. 41), God allowed the nations to walk in their own ways (Acts 14:16). Therefore, we should not read every detail of world history as if it were plotted in advance by God as part of a master plan. Instead we should think of the nations as stumbling around in the darkness.

As long as the nations live in darkness without catching sight of the great light provided by God, their history can have no ultimate, abiding significance. All they have built and achieved is destined to perish — unlike the works of those who live and die in the Lord. *"Blessed are the dead who die in the Lord,"* says a voice from heaven in one of John's visions. The Spirit adds that they are *"blessed indeed,"* since *"they may rest from their labors, for their deeds follow them"* (Revelation 14:13). No such satisfaction is allowed the nations as they stumble about in the darkness. The nations do nothing with their freedom.

Finally, believers, those whom God calls to be part of His Kingdom, are allowed a measure of freedom in this sense. God does not immediately admit them to full communion with Him; to a certain extent, He still leaves them to themselves and keeps His distance.

Even when they catch sight of their task and realize how that task contributes to the building of the Lord's Kingdom, He often lets them work out the details for themselves, giving them no more specific guidance than is provided by His law and His Word in Scripture. The Bible's emphasis falls on *responsibility*. The believer knows that his works will abide. Therefore he must work while it is yet day (John 9:4).

Nowhere in Scripture is the responsibility of the believer made more obvious than in the parable of the talents (Matthew 25:14ff). Life in the covenant is not simply a matter of taking orders from the senior covenant partner. The master goes away — here we have "distance" again — and entrusts different talents to each servant. But he makes the same demand of each one: do something with those talents! It's up to you!

In this parable we find freedom and divine direction combined. The divine direction is very general in this case, but we know from other passages of Scripture that God usually has specific, concrete aims in mind, and that He achieves them either with man's help or despite his opposition.

But if God always gets His way in the end, what are we to make of man's freedom and responsibility? Don't we have to choose theologically between divine direction and human freedom?

This problem, of which theologians have made so much, is not as great an obstacle to understanding the Bible as many people seem to think. If I want someone to do what I have in mind, I can either *order* him to do it or so arrange things that he winds up doing it of his own volition. The Bible gives us an example of this: Rebekah wanted Isaac to give the blessing of the first-born to Jacob. If she had *ordered* Isaac to do so, or simply asked him, he would most likely have refused. Therefore she *tricked* him into doing it. That way her will was done!

God, likewise, can either order man to do His will or so arrange things that His will is done without man knowing what God's purpose is. In either case man is choosing freely, just as Isaac was free when he gave the blessing of the first-born to the son who appeared before him with meat prepared.

The story of Joseph in Egypt gives us another example: Joseph was hated by his brothers, who freely chose to get rid of him in a sinful manner — by selling him to slavetraders on their way to Egypt. But God was at work behind the scenes, accomplishing His purposes. Joseph pointed this out when he finally revealed his identity to his startled brothers in Egypt: *"God sent me here before you to preserve for you a remnant on earth, and to keep alive for you many survivors. So it was not you who sent me here, but God"* (Genesis 45:7-8).

The Bible does not recognize a strict separation between the deeds of men and God's actions as He works out His purposes. We see this reflected in how the Israelites were given the land of Canaan. The Lord Himself would drive out the Canaanites. This promise came to the Israelites repeatedly, and in colorful detail: *"Behold, I will drive out before you the Amorites, the Canaanites, the Hittites, the Perizzites, the Hivites, and the Jebusites"* (Exodus 34:11). But this did not mean that the people of Israel were exempted from taking up the sword. They still had to fight many a bloody battle, and they did not all survive the warfare to enjoy the promised land.

The intertwining of God's purposes and human events is reflected beautifully in the book of Esther, the book that does not even mention the name of God. In the first part of the book we are told of a series of events leading up to a Jewish woman's elevation to the throne alongside King Ahasuerus. Then comes the threat to the survival of the Jews. Mordecai pleads with Queen Esther to do something: *"Who knows whether you have not come to the kingdom for such a time as this?"* (4:14). Indeed, this must have been the purpose, as we see from the outcome of the story. Human beings pursue their own goals as God works out His purposes.

The proper use of our freedom, of course, is obedience and service. Freedom can all too easily lead us to become enslaved to sin, which is the bondage of which Paul speaks (Romans 6:15ff). Instead, we must be slaves to righteousness and obedience, allowing God to work out His purposes in and through our lives as we follow the path of obedience. Indeed, obedience is the highest kind of freedom.

The truth does make us free (John 8:32, 36), but we are free to *serve.* Divine direction and human freedom ultimately blend in the history of salvation in the form of obedient service. God may use the nations to chastise Israel, but such "rods" are later cast aside. Only those who serve His purposes in freedom and love are kept for His own.

"You were called to freedom," Paul writes, *"only do not use your freedom as an opportunity for the flesh, but through love be servants of one another"* (Galatians 5:13). That's how we make history — the abiding history of the Kingdom of God!

7

The History of Revelation

Many Christians like to characterize the history recorded in Scripture as redemptive history or the history of salvation. As we saw in Chapter 2, this characterization is somewhat too limited, for various reasons. First of all, the history of man before the fall into sin hardly fits under the umbrella of redemptive history. Secondly, if we shift the focus from man and his plight to God and His honor and glory, we see that biblical history is also to be viewed as the history of revelation.

The purpose of the written history in Scripture is not just to tell us how man is saved; it is intended to reveal God to us. Therefore we must learn to read the Bible as a book of *revelational* history. God uses history to make Himself known to man.

People who are theologically inclined sometimes ask themselves how it is possible for God in all His majesty to reveal Himself to such a creature as fallen man. They eventually come to the realization that God "accommodates" Himself to us by presenting Himself in simple terms that *we* can understand. That's why Scripture is so full of anthropomorphisms; that is, passages in which God is spoken of as though He were a human being.

The truth about God is too immense for man to grasp. It must be presented in the same sort of childlike manner that parents and teachers often use when teaching difficult lessons to small children. God must bend down, come down to our level, speak our language, and show Himself to us within our limited horizon. This He does within history.

There is another reason why God uses history to reveal Himself to us. A great deal is revealed about Him in the Bible — enough for a well-developed "theo-logy" (teaching about God). But if all that theology were presented to man in well-defined abstract categories of the sort that systematic theologians like to use, it's not likely that we would be able to grasp it or understand it. Therefore, God stays away from any abstract approach.

The approach He uses instead is not so different from what you or I often do when we introduce ourselves to others. If you're seated next to someone on a long train trip and you get into a serious conversation, you may be asked to identify yourself. If the person you're talking to really wants to know who you are, you may tell him the outline of your life story — where you were born, what you studied in school, what sort of work you've done since then, how many children you have, what your hopes for the future are, and so forth. God introduces Himself in much the same way.

When the Lord gives His people His law, He does not talk about His communicable and incommunicable attributes. He says simply: *"I am the Lord your God, who brought you out of the land of Egypt, out of the house of bondage"* (Exodus 20:2). That was the first thing every Israelite had to know about God. But there was much more, of course. Psalm 78 is a virtual catalogue of God's deeds and accomplishments; it lists *"the glorious deeds of the Lord, and his might, and the wonders which he has wrought"* (Verse 4).

Some modern thinkers claim that we can never really know what a person is like "inside." All we can know is what he does and what he has done. Whether or not this theory is true, it can hardly be denied that we do in fact get to know people through their actions. And so it is with God.

Because there is so much to know about God, we need a very long book to record His actions. If we didn't have the Bible to tell us about God's deeds, we wouldn't know Him as well as

He wants us to know Him.

Great truths are hard to swallow and digest in one bite. This is the principle that makes the history of revelation necessary. We get to know God in stages, filling in more and more details of the picture as time goes by and we deepen our familiarity with His revelation of Himself in history.

Teachers will recognize a sound pedagogical principle here. Difficult ideas should be presented more than once, at different levels of complexity. This teaching principle is used by God throughout the history of revelation.

Shortly after the fall, God presented man with a glorious promise about redemption (Genesis 3:15). The people who received the promise did not know exactly what it meant and how it would be worked out. We, who read that promise in the light of later redemptive history, sometimes assume too quickly that it was clear and easy to understand. The fact is that the promise needed further explanation and elaboration; and that's just what it got, in the rest of biblical history.

It was a promise of deliverance from sin and its power. But how could God's people be shown what deliverance means? They found out when their covenant partner led them out of bondage in Egypt in breathtaking fashion.

But that deliverance was only temporary, and provisional. Time and again in later history, God's people had to cry out for deliverance, and each fresh occurrence brought to them a fuller understanding of what their ultimate deliverance through the Redeemer would involve. The promise became richer and more complete as it was repeated and refined. Bit by bit God's people got the message — at least, those who really wanted to get it.

As we consider the unfolding of the promise and of God's revelation of Himself, we should recognize that the "truth" as presented to successive generations of believers was not the complete truth, with no questions left open. Because the complete truth is too immense and rich for man to grasp, believers have always had to make do with *part* of the truth. As the history of revelation progressed, more of the truth became visible, just as a mountain climber can see more and more of the terrain around him as he climbs higher and higher. We could better think of the truth presented in Scripture in terms of what we can see from a certain vantage point than in terms of what we are able to formulate in words. The full truth cannot be properly formulated within the confines of man's language.

Should it worry us that believers do not always enjoy the full truth? That we ourselves cannot claim to know the full truth? Not at all. Many of the most exemplary believers are children. Their childlike faith, which we all admire, is usually paired with a simple understanding of God and His purpose for our lives. From our lofty perch of Bible knowledge, we may tend to look down on the primitive notions of a child, but we must admit that the simple thinking that goes with this kind of faith does not hinder the child's communion with God. It's not a matter of *what* you know but of *whom* you know. To know Jesus Christ is to have eternal life (I John 5:20).

Because so much is revealed to us in and through the Bible, we cannot expect to absorb all of it. Earlier generations of believers lived with a Bible that contained various errors of translation resulting from a corrupt text. (For that matter, there are probably a lot of flaws left in the modern Bible we read today.) Recent biblical scholarship has dusted off many a text and restored its meaning and therefore its place in the Bible. Yet, that Bible with its faults did not stop believers of earlier centuries from being awe-struck at the majesty of the God clearly revealed in the Bible they had before them.

We do not need every detail; we can easily do without the full truth. When it comes to God's revelation of Himself, we can only say: "My cup runneth over!" It's too much for us to take in. Even if we study the history of revelation diligently throughout our entire lives, we will never exhaust its meaning and richness.

8

Progressive Revelation

When history unfolds in the way God originally had in mind, we can speak of genuine progress. And if revelation undergoes a history, that too must be basically progressive in nature. Later revelation is based on earlier revelation and must therefore be viewed as more complete. This becomes clear especially when we examine the *promises* given to believers in the Bible.

The Bible is rich in promises — promises for us, and for the believers who lived in biblical times. When we look at Old Testament promises from a New Testament perspective, we see once again that believers generally do not have the full truth at their disposal. They may cling eagerly to certain promises and start to visualize their fulfillment, but when the fulfillment actually comes, it goes far beyond their hopes and dreams.

Biblical history gives us a good example of this pattern in what it tells us about the splendor of Solomon. As David's son and as a king ruling in the Lord's name, Solomon manifested something of God's own honor and glory. His splendor even attracted the Queen of Sheba to Jerusalem. Would Solomon live up to what she had been told about him? After inspecting Solomon's realm, the Queen declared:

The report was true which I heard in my own land of your affairs and of your wisdom, but I did not believe the reports until I came and my own eyes had seen it; and behold, half the greatness of your wisdom was not told me; you surpass the report which I heard (II Chronicles 9:5-6).

Why is this comment recorded in Scripture? Perhaps because it gives us something to think about as we ponder the promises about the day when the nations will *"beat their swords into plow-shares, and their spears into pruning hooks"* (Micah 4:3; Isaiah 2:4).

Relying again on a visual comparison, we could say that progressive revelation is like a hiker walking toward a landmark in the distance. The first form of the promise is his first glimpse of the landmark on the horizon. As he advances toward it, he catches sight of more and more details. His first impression of it is superseded when he finally stands before the landmark and inspects it close up. *"When I was a child, I spoke like a child, I thought like a child, I reasoned like a child,"* explains Paul. *"When I became a man, I gave up childish ways. For now we see in a mirror dimly, but then face to face"* (I Corinthians 13:11-12).

Of all the saints in Scripture, there was no one who knew this better than Abraham, the recipient of the promise that led to the formation of the covenant community. Abraham is called the father of all believers, for we are all his spiritual offspring. But he is also the father of believers in the sense that he sets an example for us. If anyone ever had to live by faith, it was Abraham. When he was *"as good as dead"* (Hebrews 11:12), he was told that he would become the father of a great nation!

Abraham lived by the promise, then. And the promise came to him repeatedly. When he was seventy-five years old, the Lord said to him:

Go from your country and your kindred and your father's house to the land that I will show you. And I will make of you a great nation, and I will bless you, and make your name great, so that you will be a blessing. I will bless those who bless you, and him who curses you I will curse; and by you all the families of the earth shall bless themselves (Genesis 12:1-3).

This promise was really one of redemption: redemption was somehow to come through Abraham and his descendants. That he would have many descendants was part of the promise.

When Abraham got to Canaan, the Lord came to him for the second time with the promise: *"To your descendants I will give this land"* (Genesis 12:7). Now the promise was made more specific. Abraham's descendants would have a land of their own — Canaan!

After Abraham parted company with Lot, the Lord came to him for the third time to talk about the promise. Abraham then found out that his descendants would hold their land forever and that they would be as the dust of the earth — innumerable (Genesis 13:14-17).

Abraham still did not have a son. How, then, could the promise be fulfilled? Again the Lord appeared to him. This time He promised Abraham a son and declared that his descendants would be as numerous as the stars of the heavens. The Lord went on to tell Abraham that there would be four hundred years of oppression in a foreign land before his descendants took possession of their land. He also promised that Abraham would die in peace (Genesis 15).

The promise came to Abraham for the fifth time when he was ninety-nine years old. He was now told that he would be the father of a *"multitude of nations."* Moreover, God would be the God of those descendants: *"And I will establish my covenant between me and you and your descendants after you throughout their generations for an everlasting covenant, to be God to you and to your descendants after you."* The sign of that covenant would be circumcision. There was more: Abraham's aged wife Sarah was to be a mother of nations. Despite her age, she would bear Abraham a son named Isaac, with whom God would establish His covenant (Genesis 17).

The sixth time the Lord came to Abraham with the promise, He told him that Sarah would give birth to her baby within about a year (Genesis 18:10-14). After this comes the shameful Abimelech episode, when Abraham gives up his wife in fear, just as he had done years before in Egypt. All the same, he gets her back and Isaac is born on schedule.

When Abraham demonstrates his willingness to sacrifice Isaac, the Lord comes to him for the seventh time with the promise, this time summing it up and confirming it:

> *I will indeed bless you, and I will multiply your descendants as the stars of heaven and as the sand which is on the seashore. And your descendants shall possess the gate of their enemies, and by your descendants shall all the nations of the earth bless themselves* (Genesis 22:17-18).

How much did this tell Abraham about the later history of salvation? The final form of the promise was hardly a detailed prophecy. All the same, Jesus was able to say of Abraham: *"Your father Abraham rejoiced that he was to see my day; he saw it and was glad"* (John 8:56). The book of Hebrews testifies of Abraham that he *"looked forward to the city which has foundations, whose builder and maker is God"* (Hebrews 11:10).

The promise was gradually made more specific, but Abraham was not given the details. Even so, he looked forward to the coming of the Redeemer and the completion of the work of redemption.

The promise that comes to God's people repeatedly in Scripture can also be read as the promise of a *king*. And just what is a king in God's redemptive plan? Psalm 72 tells us. The psalmist prays:

> *Give the king thy justice, O God,*
> *and thy righteousness to the royal son!*
> *May he judge thy people with righteousness,*
> *and thy poor with justice!*
> *May he defend the cause of the poor of the people,*
> *give deliverance to the needy,*
> *and crush the oppressor!* (Verses 1-2, 4).

Israel's king was to give his people a foretaste of their complete deliverance through the Redeemer.

That the king was really supposed to point ahead to the Redeemer becomes clear later in the psalm:

May his name endure for ever,
his fame continue as long as the sun!
May men bless themselves by him,
all nations call him blessed! (Verse 17).

Without a king to establish justice and righteouness, things go wrong and wickedness abounds. This became obvious in the period of the judges. In the book of Judges, which gives us some divine commentary on the events of those days, we read repeatedly: *"In those days there was no king in Israel; every man did what was right in his own eyes."*

A king was part of God's plan for Israel all along. In fact, God in effect promised Israel a king when He provided laws to govern the king's conduct (Deuteronomy 17). The king was to rule by the law of the Lord and thereby make the Lord's righteousness known to his people.

Saul, Israel's first king, did not do so. With Saul things went wrong from the start, for the people had come begging to Samuel for *"a king to govern us like all the nations"* (I Samuel 8:5). Samuel tried to dissuade them, but they insisted: *"We will have a king over us, that we also may be like all the nations, and that our king may govern us and go out before us and fight our battles"* (Verses 19-20).

Saul's kingship was not a step ahead in the progressive unfolding of God's revelation of Himself, but David's was. Because the Lord was pleased with David, He deepened the redemptive purpose of the kingship through a promise made to him: *"And your house and your kingship shall be made sure for ever before me; your throne shall be established for ever"* (II Samuel 7:16; I Chronicles 17:14). This promise was renewed when Solomon found favor in God's eyes: *"I will establish your royal throne over Israel for ever, as I promised David your father"* (I Kings 9:5; II Chronicles 7:18).

We all know what happened afterward. David's house went into decline, and the kingdom was torn in two. Eventually the princes of David's house went into exile. Yet, God fulfilled the promise to David in the kingship of David's Son, Jesus Christ. And that fulfillment is far more glorious than the prospect of a restoration of the Davidic kingdom with Solomon's splendor.

Even Jesus' own disciples were slow to understand this point. *"Lord, will you at this time restore the kingdom to Israel?"* they asked Him just before His ascension (Acts 1:6). They still had not caught on.

The truths the Bible wants to teach us take a long time to sink in. This we discover from our own reading of biblical history. Because it takes so long, God makes it easier for us by presenting the truth of redemption in a history book — the history of salvation through the covenant, which is at the same time the ever-progressing history of revelation.

If we are to get the full picture concerning our salvation — the picture God wants us to get — we must study that history from cover to cover, going through it repeatedly and discussing the material thoroughly. And if we hope to *"grow in the grace and knowledge of our Lord and Savior Jesus Christ"* (II Peter 3:18), we must *make progress* in our study of God's revelation.

9

Reading the Bible as History

When we come across history in the Bible, we should read it as such instead of searching for some hidden meaning "behind" the narrative. What we read in the Bible is really world history, for it deals with the origin and destiny of the entire human race. Because of the fall into sin, however, the history of the human race has taken on a certain specific character: it is redemptive history, the account of salvation and judgment within the framework of the covenant. At the same time we must learn to read biblical history as revelational history, in which God makes Himself known to man step by step.

The Bible, then, gives us a record of the history of salvation and revelation and must be read in the light of this primary intent. But what does this mean in practical terms? How are we to go about it?

To begin with, we must avoid the error of "dispensationalism." Dispensationalism might look like a beautiful presentation of redemptive history, but it is actually anti-historical in character, for it denies the unity and continuity of God's dealings with man throughout history.

What is dispensationalism? At the very least, it is an effort to take account of the fact that there are *stages* in God's redemptive plan. We all know that the sacrificial death and subsequent resurrection of Jesus Christ is the great turning point in history. We even speak of an "old covenant" and a "new covenant," echoing the Bible's own language (Jeremiah 31:31-4). But the dispensationalists go much further. They identify a number of strictly separate periods in God's dealings with man — as many as seven. In each of those periods, they tell us, God deals with man on different terms.

The result of this misleading teaching is that we lose sight of the centrality of God's grace. Remember that the Old Testament believers were saved by grace just as we are today. And they were called to live by the same law of love that holds for us today. Where we differ from them is that we can look back on so much more fulfillment of God's redemptive promises, and that frees us from Old Testament ceremonial requirements. We enjoy the fruits of Christ's finished work and the benefits of the outpouring of the Holy Spirit.

Dispensationalism undermines the Old Testament's status as Scripture as well as the status of the church. And it often leads to speculation about the last things because it ignores the covenant and therefore misreads much of biblical prophecy. If the emphasis on redemptive history led to an espousal of dispensationalism, then, we would have to stay far away from it.

Fortunately, there are much better ways of reading biblical history as redemptive history, ways that emphasize continuity rather than discontinuity. "New Testament Christians" who like to put all the stories and laws and prophecies of the Old Testament behind them as they concentrate on the "new deal" preached by Jesus should pay careful attention to what Jesus Himself said. Jesus did not address Himself to the Jews only; He also went to the Samaritans. Still, He declared that *"salvation is from the Jews"* (John 4:22), that is, that it comes to all mankind by way of the Jewish people. By Abraham's seed, all the nations of the earth were to be blessed.

The Jews enjoyed a certain primacy in the plan of redemptive history. Paul spoke of the gospel as *"the power of God for salvation to every one who has faith, to* the Jew first *and also to the Greek"* (Romans 1:16). That's why he made it a point to preach in the Jewish synagogues when he went on his missionary journeys outside Palestine.

The continuity in redemptive history is made possible by the covenant. When God decided to send the Redeemer into the world and gather a people as His special possession (Exodus 19:5), He did so through the covenant. Redemptive history is a unity because it is covenant history.

Covenant history is at the same time the context within which we are to read revelational history. God wanted to reveal the Redeemer bit by bit before He came. The Redeemer is the covenant head of God's elect. Therefore, one way to make the Redeemer known was to give believers a glimpse of what He would do for them and be to them through what the office-bearers within the covenant framework said and did.

We must learn to look at the judges, kings, prophets, priests, and family heads of the Old Testament as previews of the Christ. Here, too, we find continuity rather than discontinuity. Jesus did not come to teach His people that the Old Testament is too negative, too concerned with judgment, too preoccupied with law. No, He came to fulfill what the Old Testament taught concerning Him, and He pointed this out repeatedly.

If continuity is the key — rather than the discontinuity emphasized by dispensationalists — what guidelines can we use to make sure that our reading of biblical history respects its character as redemptive history and revelational history? What approach must we take if we are to rule out the tendency to read biblical history as a series of edifying stories and legends that could just as well be fables as factual accounts? In other words, what must we look for in biblical narratives if we reject the hypothesis that the Bible can best be read as a series of parables and fables intended to aid us in our moral development?

The first guideline is that we must *keep our eyes fixed on the continuing covenant line leading toward the fulfillment of God's promise of a Redeemer.*

This guideline often helps us understand why a given story is in the Bible. In Genesis 38, for example, we read about a sordid series of events that most story Bibles consider unsuitable for telling to children. What is this chapter doing in the Bible?

We find part of the answer on the opening page of the New Testament. Perez, the son of Judah born as a result of the sorry history related in Genesis 38, is one of the ancestors of David and thereby of the Christ. On his deathbed Jacob had special words of praise for Judah (Genesis 49:8-12), but we see that this honor was bestowed on him because of God's election — and not because of any exemplary behavior on Judah's part. The story recorded in Genesis 38 underscores God's sovereign grace in election, even in the case of the Redeemer's ancestry.

Joseph's "rags to riches" adventures in Egypt may seem edifying, but they are also to be read in the light of this guideline. God was taking steps to preserve the covenant community, the line from which the Christ would be born. He had told Abraham that his descendants would undergo a four-hundred-year period of preparation for what awaited them (Genesis 15:13-14), and he used Joseph as a channel to lead the history of the covenant line in that direction. The point of the story is not Joseph's heroism and courage but God's plan, as Joseph himself testified (Genesis 45:5ff; 50:19-20).

As we follow this line through biblical history, we must not get carried away and say that God could *only* implement His plan by having Joseph go to Egypt as a slave. The Bible does not tell us any such thing. All it tells us is that it pleased God to bring deliverance to His people by this route. For all we know, God could have used entirely different means and channels. The important thing is what actually happened — not what might have been.

The second guideline is that we must *look at certain persons and events in biblical history as prefigurations and foreshadowings of the Redeemer*. The king is not just a king, and the priest is not just a priest. Because the king ruled over God's people within the framework of the covenant, his bearing and conduct were intended to give believers an advance peek at the Messiah.

Therefore the king placed on the throne by God was to be regarded not just as the king but also as a forerunner of the Redeemer. God's own honor was bound up with the king's honor. This applies only to the king within the covenant community, of course. God also used the kings of foreign nations to carry out His purposes: think of Cyrus, who gave permission for the exiled Jews to return to their own land (II Chronicles 36:22-3; Ezra 1:1-4; Isaiah 44:28). But those foreign kings did not reflect the King who was to come.

David was well aware of the special significance of Israel's king. Therefore he held his followers back when they wanted to kill Saul, who was making things so difficult for them. Saul, he reminded them, was *"the Lord's anointed"* (I Samuel 24:3-6; 26:8-11). But David himself did not fare as well at the hands of Shimei, who appeared on the scene during Absalom's rebellion. David's sin with Bathsheba had led to judgment: Nathan prophesied that the sword would never depart from his house. Absalom's rebellion was the most dramatic fulfillment of that judgment.

David was forced to flee from Jerusalem in order to gain time to build up forces to resist Absalom. In a mournful procession, Israel's king and some soldiers and followers faithful to him left Jerusalem. On the way they were confronted by Shimei, a member of Saul's house. Shimei threw stones at David's party and cursed the king: *"The Lord has avenged upon you all the blood of the house of Saul, in whose place you have reigned; and the Lord has given the kingdom into the hand of your son Absalom"* (II Samuel 16:8).

Abishai, one of David's officers, wanted to kill Shimei, but David would not let him. In his anxiety and depression, he assumed that *the Lord* had sent Shimei to curse him. What he overlooked was that the Lord's own name was being defamed at the same time, for David was now "the Lord's anointed."

When Absalom was defeated, Shimei realized that his life was in danger. Therefore, he immediately went to David to beg forgiveness. Abishai again urged David not to take this matter lightly: *"Shall not Shimei be put to death for this, because he cursed the Lord's anointed?"* (II Samuel 19:21). But David, who was in a generous mood after his victory, again said no. Now that he was out of danger, he felt that he could overlook Shimei's offense against the Lord's name.

Toward the end of his life, David was bothered about the mistake he had made with regard to Shimei. Before he died, he spoke to Solomon about this piece of unfinished business: *"Now therefore hold him not guiltless, for you are a wise man; you will know what you ought to do to him, and you shall bring down his gray head with blood to Sheol"* (I Kings 2:9). But even Solomon hesitated. Instead of executing Shimei, he confined him to Jerusalem. Shimei violated the king's orders and was finally put to death (Verses 36-46).

Story Bibles usually tell how Shimei cursed David, but they generally omit the rest of the story. They make the same mistake that David himself made: they fail to recognize Israel's king as "the Lord's anointed," the forerunner of the Redeemer, and God's channel for revealing something of the Redeemer's glory.

The third guideline is that we must *always be careful to take the stage or phase in the unfolding of redemptive history into account.*

While God always deals with His own on the basis of the covenant of *grace,* things do change because of events within redemptive history. Hence we must learn to put situations and controversies within their redemptive historical context. What applies to believers at an earlier stage in redemptive history may not apply to us today.

An example is the relationship of Christianity to Judaism. A Christian does not participate in worship services in a Jewish synagogue any more than he joins Muslims or Buddhists in worship. The Jews do not confess the name of Christ. And we know that *"every spirit which does not confess Jesus is not of God"* (I John 4:3). The Judaistic denial that Jesus is the Messiah makes it impossible for Christians to look upon orthodox Jews as brothers in the faith.

This might seem clear-cut, but when we open the Bible we see that it was not quite so simple for the early church. The first believers, who were Jews, continued to worship in the temple after Jesus' crucifixion and ascension (Acts 2:46). Even Peter and John went to the temple *"at the hour of prayer"* (Acts 3:1). A number of years later we also find Paul in the temple in Jerusalem (Acts 21:26; 24:18). He was accused of defiling the temple by bringing in a Gentile, but it turned out that this accusation was unfounded.

How could the early Christians continue to worship in the temple? Didn't the services in the temple become superfluous once Jesus died and rose again? After all, the great veil in the temple was torn in two at the moment of His death (Matthew 27:51). God was no longer present on earth through the temple but through the victorious Christ, and later through the Holy Spirit poured out on His church.

Christ's body took the place of the temple, as He Himself explained at the time of the temple cleansing. In Luke's account we read simply that Jesus complained that the temple had been made a den of robbers instead of a house of prayer (Luke 19:45-6). But John talks of an earlier temple cleansing in which Jesus remarked: *"Destroy this temple, and in three days I will raise it up"* (John 2:19). The Jews misunderstood Jesus, and so John explains to his readers: *"But he spoke of the temple of his body"* (Verse 21).

If the completion of Jesus' work (rebuilding the temple of His body in three days) made the temple superfluous, what were His followers up to in the temple? Didn't they realize that they could have no fellowship with Jews who refused to confess the name of Jesus?

They must have known this, but at the same time they recognized that these stubborn Jews were members of the covenant people. As such they were not yet excluded by God. The Messiah had indeed come, but they would first be given time to recognize Him. If they didn't acknowledge Him as the Messiah, the covenant wrath of which the Old Testament spoke (see Deuteronomy 28:15-68) would strike them. And that was just what happened.

Jesus Himself prophesied about the covenant wrath that was to strike Jerusalem and the temple because of the refusal of the Jews to recognize the Christ:

O Jerusalem, Jerusalem, killing the prophets and stoning those who are sent to you! How often would I have gathered your children together as a hen gathers her brood under her wings, and you would not! Behold, your house is forsaken. And I tell you, you will not see me until you say, "Blessed is he who comes in the name of the Lord" (Luke 13:34-5; 19:41ff).

On His way to Golgotha He said:

Daughters of Jerusalem, do not weep for me, but weep for yourselves and for your children. For behold, the days are coming when they will say, "Blessed are the barren, and the wombs that never bore, and the breasts that never gave suck!" Then they will begin to say to the mountains, "Fall on us"; and to the hills, "Cover us" (Luke 23:28-30).

Jesus had made the same point earlier to His disciples. Pointing to the temple He told them: *"The days will come when there shall not be left here one stone upon another that will not be thrown down"* (Luke 21:6; Matthew 24:1ff; Mark 13:1ff).

That day did indeed come — when Jerusalem and the temple were destroyed in A.D. 70. The horrible destruction was God's judgment on the Jews who refused to accept the Messiah sent under the terms of the covenant. Those Jews were guilty of the worst possible form of covenant breaking: they rejected the Redeemer whose coming was the fulfillment of the heart of the covenant promise.

The temple was never reestablished, and the Jews never regained their status as God's covenant people. Now the Jews can enter the covenant as believers in Christ only on the same terms as the Gentiles. That's why their worship services in the synagogues are no place for a Christian.

In the period of grace *before* the destruction of Jerusalem, however, there could still be some fellowhip and communion between believers of the old covenant and believers of the new. The visits to the temple recorded in Acts are entirely understandable when placed in their redemptive historical context.

The fourth guideline is that we must *endeavor to understand the major characters in the Bible in terms of their place in the history of salvation.*

This is important, especially when we consider the stories about Jesus. Jesus did not come into the world in the first place to present Himself to us as an example to be followed. Therefore we should not say that it is our goal to imitate the conduct of Jesus and to react in every situation as Jesus would have reacted.

If we shared in Jesus' calling as the Redeemer sent into the world, we could feel obliged to follow in His footsteps — but we don't. Instead of imitating Jesus, we must live as He taught us to live. To His disciples He said: *"If you love me, you will keep my commandments"* (John 14:15).

Paul once appealed to the Christians of Corinth to be imitators: *"Be imitators of me, as I am of Christ"* (I Corinthians 11:1; I Thessalonians 1:6). Thus, there is a sense in which we must strive to be Christ-like — using Paul, the *"foremost of sinners,"* as he called himself (I Timothy 1:15), as our model. We imitate Christ in the style of Paul by following Christ — but not by trying to speak and act with His divine authority, or developing any messianic aspirations and illusions. It was not Jesus' mission on earth to set an example for us.

This is a difficult point for many Christians to accept. The idea of Jesus as the great example to be followed in all situations is deeply rooted in both the churches and the secular culture of our time. Indeed, it is one of the points on which many Christians and unbelievers seem to be able to agree. Yet, this agreement is not rooted in Scripture.

Jesus did not come to earth to do good deeds and thereby inspire us to do the same. On one occasion He did deliberately set an example for His disciples, but then He made it explicit what He was doing (John 13:1ff). He spoke in democratic language about all believers being equal, but at the same time He emphasized His own office: *"Call no man your father on earth, for you have one Father, who is in heaven. Neither be called masters, for you have one master, the Christ"* (Matthew 23:9-10).

We like to picture Jesus as a teacher by example, one who gave water to the thirsty and bread to the hungry. He did indeed give water to the thirsty, but even then His office and calling were uppermost in His mind. When He met the Samaritan woman at Jacob's well, He offered her water — the water of eternal life (John 4:7-15). The emphasis fell on His work of redemption — and not on "good deeds."

Thus we are not to think of Jesus as someone who set an example that we must follow constantly. Remember that Jesus was criticized for spending time with disreputable people and notorious sinners. Why did He do so? To set an example for us? When His enemies questioned Him on this point, He emphasized His *calling* again: those sinners needed a physician (Matt. 9:10ff; Mark 2:16-17; Luke 5:29ff).

On one occasion He sent his disciples on a curious mission: they were to go to a certain house unannounced and take away a colt tethered there. Again, He was not setting an example or suggesting that we should do the same sort of thing every now and then. If the disciples were challenged, they were simply to say: "The Lord *has need of it"* (Mark 11:3; Matthew 21:3; Luke 19:31).

We can understand the words and deeds of Jesus properly only in their context in redemptive history. Jesus emphasized that He was sent into the world for a certain purpose and that He had come in the Father's name (John 5:43). And what was that purpose?

> *I have come down from heaven, not to do my own will, but the will of him who sent me; and this is the will of him who sent me, that I should lose nothing of all that he has given me, but raise it up at the last day. For this is the will of my Father, that every one who sees the Son and believes in him should have eternal life; and I will raise him up at the last day* (John 6:38-40).

Jesus' mission as Savior is the key to understanding the stories about Him. Nowhere does this come through more directly than in the story of the costly ointment spread over His feet shortly before His crucifixion. Couldn't the money for that ointment have been better given to the poor? That was the question raised by Judas, and he seemed to have a good point there. Jesus responded by way of a famous sentence that is often misused: *"The poor you always have with you, but you do not always have me"* (John 12:8). The emphasis here is not that the poor are unimportant and should be overlooked, but that *Jesus* is all-important. He is the Savior and King to whom all honor is due.

10

Samples and Examples

We saw earlier that biblical history is misinterpreted if it is not viewed as redemptive history. Jesus was not just a teacher of religion and morals, and David was not just an earthly king. Samson was much more than a national hero, and Abraham is not to be reduced to a nonconformist with a dream of his own. All these biblical characters occupy special places in the history of salvation and can only be properly understood in terms of their position in that history.

Once we have grasped this point, we have made considerable progress toward understanding the narratives in the Bible as *history*; that is, as a record of events. We are then reading biblical history as its authors intended it to be read. But we are not yet done with the Bible when we understand it on this level.

We read the Bible as a history book in an effort to become familiar with the history of salvation, but we also read it because it has a message for each one of us today. How can history bring us a personal message?

It is on this point that many Christians have problems with a redemptive historical approach to Scripture. They may recognize the validity of such an emphasis in biblical scholarship and exegesis, but they do not see how a redemptive historical approach opens up the personal message that the Bible is supposed to bring each of us as citizens of the Western world living two thousand years after the time of Christ.

Scholars who study preaching and biblical interpretation have a name for this problem: it is the problem of *application*. When one has discovered the historical meaning of a text, the text has then been explained, or *explicated*. But the question remains: How is the text to be *applied* to our lives today? Preachers who pick historical texts often have difficulty bringing a sermon to a conclusion because they do not know how to relate the episode they are discussing to twentieth-century life.

One route preachers have all too often taken in the face of this difficulty is to assume that the episodes in biblical history are recorded to supply us with moral lessons and examples. The story of David and Goliath teaches us self-confidence. David's refusal to kill Saul when Saul falls into his hands teaches us to respect people in positions of authority. The attack of the bears on the boys at Bethel who jeered at the prophet Elisha shows us the importance of good manners. Saul's refusal to wait for Samuel before the battle against the Philistines teaches us patience. Some story Bibles even provide indexes to tell us which stories illustrate which virtues!

This approach to Bible stories has often been criticized — and rightly so. When David took on Goliath, an important element in the story was the abuse Goliath heaped on *the name of the Lord.* When David refused to kill Saul, it was because he realized that *the Lord* had placed Saul on Israel's throne and would remove him when David's time came. When the boys of Bethel made fun of Elisha, they were rejecting *the Word of the Lord,* which enjoyed little respect in Bethel, that center of idolatry. And when Saul went ahead with the sacrifice instead of waiting for Samuel, he was violating the distinction between the offices of priest and king, a distinction established by *the Lord.*

The realization that a moral lesson is not primarily what the stories in biblical history are intended to teach us (otherwise we could preach on legends and myths from all over the world) has led some preachers to insist that any effort to "apply" such stories by looking to them for examples is illegitimate. In the Netherlands there has been a lively debate between those who believe that it is permitted to draw moral "examples" from biblical history (the exemplary approach) and those who sought applications purely in terms of the history of salvation (the redemptive historical approach). This debate, which ended quite some time ago, resulted in extreme statements on both sides, but it did illustrate the importance of looking at redemptive history as the framework and context even in our *applications* of Scripture passages in which biblical history is recorded.

That lesson is the legacy of the debate. Yet the debate itself is misleading in that it seems to suggest that a redemptive historical approach to Scripture leaves no room for looking at the episodes in Scripture as "examples." This is not so; the strong moral emphasis that has traditionally characterized Christian preaching need not be abandoned because of a commitment to a redemptive historical reading of Scripture.

The important point to note here is that many of the stories recorded in Scripture provide examples that go *beyond* the usual moral emphasis. Such stories are exemplary in a broader sense, for they teach us general truths about God's dealings with man within the covenantal framework of the history of salvation. They give us examples of the riches that God's redemption brings us. To make the point clearer, we could speak of those examples as "samples."

The coming of the Redeemer and the completion of His redemptive work was to bring God's people peace and justice. In the Old Testament, God's people were given many an example — or sample — of what lay ahead. In the reign of a king like David, they could taste something of the glory of the coming Messiah, of whom David was a "type" or reflection. Even in the destructive fury of a judge like Samson they could get a glimpse of what was to come — judgment and deliverance. Thus we can attach a certain exemplary significance to David, Samson, and many of the other Old Testament characters who were called to reflect the Redeemer's justice and mercy, and even to the tablernacle as a foreshadowing of God's promise to be with His people again.

Those who wish to deal with biblical history only as a storehouse of moral examples often object that a redemptive historical approach to application leaves the imagination too free. Don't we wind up reading all sorts of things into biblical history that are not really there? If the authors of the Old Testament books knew about the Messiah only through promise and prophecy, how could they reflect Him in their depiction of the characters they presented?

This question is not so difficult to answer if we remember that God Himself is the ultimate author of Scripture. When we study the Bible, we must proceed on the assumption that the human author often did not realize the full significance of what he was writing. Was the author of Genesis fully aware of the striking parallel between Abraham's willingness to sacrifice his beloved son on the altar and God's willingness to sacrifice His beloved Son to cleanse us from our sins? Probably not.

The Bible amazes us time and again because of all the interrelations between its many parts. We cannot help but be struck by the care with which it was composed. God Himself had a hand in this. How else could the writings of so many separate individuals over so many centuries combine to form a harmonious whole?

Earlier we distinguished between the events of redemptive history, the record of those events, and the divine commentary on that record (pp. 12, 13). On all three levels, God's guidance is the key to understanding biblical history as redemptive history.

First of all, God saw to it that certain Old Testament events and characters brought to light something of what the Christ would accomplish. Then He made sure that the Messianic and prophetic side of biblical history was recognizable in the written account. Finally, to that written record He added some commentary about His own involvement, to make sure that the readers of Scripture would understand that those Messianic flashes were not accidents, but were intended as a revelation of what lay ahead and a guarantee that the promise was and is sure.

Yet, even if we emphasize God's own hand in the composition of Scripture, we must admit that there is a danger of getting carried away when it comes to looking for redemptive historical applications of the episodes in biblical history. Therefore, we must follow certain guidelines. But where are those guidelines to be found?

We find them in Scripture itself. The New Testament leads the way when it comes to applying the Bible to the lives of believers centuries later.

The applications generally fall into two groups. First of all there are incidents in redemptive history that reveal the Redeemer to us, if only in a shadowy way. Jesus often drew on the Old Testament when teaching people about Himself. He pointed to a parallel between Himself and the prophet Jonah: *"For as Jonah was three days and three nights in the belly of the whale, so will the Son of man be three days and three nights in the heart of the earth"* (Matthew 12:40). Thus, when we read the story of Jonah, we should let our mind wander to what Jesus suffered before His exaltation.

Jesus also reached back to the days in the wilderness for an example to make a point about Himself: *"As Moses lifted up the serpent in the wilderness, so must the Son of man be lifted up, that whoever believes in him may have eternal life"* (John 3:14-15). The story of the bronze serpent (Numbers 21:9) is intended to teach us something about God's plan of salvation and the necessity of the cross.

The author of Hebrews makes considerable use of Old Testament history as he discusses the Christ. He draws parallels between the tabernacle under the old covenant and Christ's perfect sacrifice under the new covenant (Chapter 9). The tabernacle had its own significance and purpose for the Israelites, of course. But Hebrews makes it clear why the Bible also tells *us* about the tabernacle in such detail; the tabernacle helps us understand the meaning of Christ's redemptive work.

There is a second type of application of Old Testament history in the New Testament: parallels are drawn between the Old Testament saints and the believers under the new covenant. We are shown that the Old Testament stories should be a source of both warning and encouragement. When Paul talks about the Israelites in the wilderness, he adds: *"Now these things are warnings for us, not to desire evil as they did. . . . These things happened to them as a warning, but they were written down for our instruction"* (I Corinthians 10:6, 11).

The author of Hebrews sounds a similar warning when he points out that the rebellious Israelites stumbled in the wilderness and failed to enter the promised land themselves: *"So we see that they were unable to enter because of unbelief"* (3:19).

When Jude speaks out against the false teachers stirring up trouble among the Christians, he uses the strong language of three Old Testament parallels: *"They walk in the way of Cain, and abandon themselves for the sake of gain to Balaam's error, and perish in Korah's rebellion"* (Verse 11).

The false teachers who plagued the early church are compared by Paul to the magicians at the court of Pharaoh in the time of Moses: *"As Jannes and Jambres opposed Moses, so these men also oppose the truth"* (II Timothy 3:8).

Hebrews mentions Esau as an example of the immorality and godlessness we must stay away from (12:16), and Peter points to the example of Sarah as he counsels wives to be obedient to their husbands: *"Sarah obeyed Abraham, calling him lord. And you are now her children if you do right and let nothing terrify you"* (I Peter 3:6).

The authors of the New Testament also point to the Old Testament as a source of *comfort* for believers. Even the stories about judgment sound a note of grace and deliverance. Peter reminds his readers that God punished the cities of Sodom and Gomorrah by turning them into ashes. Yet He rescued *"righteous Lot,"* who was *"greatly distressed by the licentiousness of the wicked."* This gives us something to think about: *"The Lord knows how to rescue the godly from trial, and to keep the unrighteous under punishment until the day of judgment"* (II Peter 2:6-9).

The words of comfort that God once spoke to Elijah should also be words of comfort for us. Paul points out:

Do you not know what the scripture says of Elijah, how he pleads with God against Israel? "Lord, they have killed thy prophets, they have demolished thy altars, and I alone am left, and they seek my life." But what is God's reply to him? "I have kept for myself seven thousand men who have not bowed the knee to Baal." So too at the present time there is a remnant chosen by grace (Romans 11:2-5).

The magnificent eleventh chapter of Hebrews tells us about the role and significance of faith in the lives of the Old Testament believers. In faith those saints learned to look ahead to promises not yet fulfilled — and we must do the same:

> *By faith Moses, when he was grown up, refused to be called the son of Pharaoh's daughter, choosing rather to share ill-treatment with the people of God than to enjoy the fleeting pleasures of sin. He considered abuse suffered for the Christ greater wealth than the treasures of Egypt, for he looked to the reward* (Verses 24-6).

We must learn to do the same: suffer abuse for the sake of Christ, looking ahead to the reward that awaits us.

The New Testament points the way in applying biblical history, for it gives us quite a number of examples of how it can be done. But in our application of Old Testament history, we are not limited to the stories on which the New Testament comments directly. Using the New Testament examples as guidelines, we may confidently seek applications for our lives today, drawing comfort from the words of comfort spoken to the Old Testament Israelites, shrinking back from the sins they fell into so often, and fixing our eyes and hopes on the Redeemer they longed for. Indeed, these things were written down for our instruction — not just to satisfy our curiosity.

Jesus Christ is our *"surety of a better covenant,"* writes the author of Hebrews (7:22), showing again that the facts of redemptive history are not simply written down for the sake of information. On those facts hinges our salvation. Without the facts and events of redemptive history, our faith is in vain.

The gospel account of the Christ is not a legend with a hidden meaning; it is not a parable. *"If Christ has not been raised, then our preaching is in vain and your faith is in vain,"* Paul rightly insists (I Corinthians 15:14).

Christ's redemptive work, together with the many events that preceded it and paved the way for it, serves as an assurance for us. The episodes that make up redemptive history point ahead to what awaits us. At the same time, the actualization of the new life within the covenant community gives us a foretaste of the complete fulfillment of all God's promises. Thus we must learn to read the Bible's redemptive history as a source of assurance, keeping our eyes open for samples of what God's renewal can and will accomplish in our lives.

11

God's Law and Moralism

Some Christians like to stress the difference between a *redemptive historical* reading of Scripture and an *exemplary* approach. They do so because of their great fear of a certain danger; namely, moralism and legalism.

We have already seen that the redemptive historical emphasis and the exemplary emphasis are not complete opposites: the former contains exemplary elements. But we have not yet dealt explicitly with the relation of God's law to the flow of redemptive history. Are we to stay away from any emphasis on God's law because of the danger of moralism?

The history of Christianity in the last two centuries shows that there is good reason for concern about these matters. Many Christians in the nineteenth century assumed that Christian belief was made up of two elements: a certain moral code and a set of doctrines about the identity of a historical figure named Jesus. When the Bible's teachings about Jesus were called into question by secular scholarship, the response of many of those Christians was to insist that it made no real difference since the moral code was the heart of Christian belief. The doctrine of Christ's divinity and resurrection could safely be surrendered without affecting or undermining the Christian moral code as taught in the Bible. The result of this development was a weak-kneed liberal Protestantism, a version of Christianity that has lost ground steadily throughout the twentieth century.

One way of reacting to this development is to argue that the emphasis on the Bible's moral teachings tends to undermine our confession of Jesus as Lord and Savior. On the basis of such an outlook, we are sometimes urged not to identify the Bible's central teachings too closely with "God's law." Beware of the leaven of the moralists and legalists. The Bible is a book about redemption — not morality.

There is another development in the history of Christianity that has contributed to the lack of emphasis on "God's law," namely, the Lutheran tendency to speak of "law" and "gospel" as contrasts — or even opposites. In effect, this tendency is a form of dispensationalism, for it suggests that God deals with man on different terms in the Old Testament era than after the time of Christ. The result is that God's law is not given its proper place. Christians are "free from the law"!

This way of thinking is also unhealthy, for it undermines our respect for the state and other legitimate authority structures. We wind up looking at the law mainly as a negative, restraining force. The law/gospel contrast leaves us confused about the inherent goodness of God's law and renders us unable to join the poet of Psalm 119 in his praise for God's law:

> *If thy law had not been my delight,*
> *I should have perished in my affliction.*
> *I will never forget thy precepts;*
> *for by them thou hast given me life* (Verses 92-3).

Moralism is indeed a danger; and a false opposition between "law" and "gospel" is also to be avoided. But how does God's law fit into a redemptive historical understanding of Scripture? Is the law something that gets left behind as an earlier stage in redemptive history? Is the law as proclaimed by Moses outmoded? Has it been replaced by a higher, New Testament law?

When we seek an answer to this question, we must not overlook the fact that Jesus, too, condemned a form of "moralism" or "legalism." Think of His harsh denunciations of the Pharisees, those *"whitewashed tombs"* that appeared beautiful from the outside but were full of dead men's bones (Matthew 23:27). *"Beware of the leaven of the Pharisees,"* that is, their false teaching (Matthew 16:11-12).

What was the matter with those hypocrites? The Pharisees lived by the letter of the law: they even went far beyond it. But the spirit of the law did not concern them. *"You hypocrites! Well did Isaiah prophesy of you, when he said: 'This people honors me with their lips, but their heart is far from me'"* (Matthew 15:7-8).

The Pharisees missed the point of the law altogether; they *"neglected the weightier matters of the law, justice and mercy and faith"* (23:23). Thus the real issue was not so much what the Pharisees taught (that is, obedience to the law of Moses) but their failure to practice what they preached (Verse 3).

Ultimately the issue goes far beyond a failure to practice what you preach. Many Christians are guilty on that score, but there is forgiveness for such a failing. The Pharisees were denounced so strongly because they thought they could *earn their salvation* by keeping the law. They spurned God's redemptive plan as it was realized in history, choosing instead to seek salvation on their own. Hence their eyes were not open to recognize the Redeemer when He came. And that was a direct affront to God.

Scripture is emphatic on the question of earning one's salvation. *"We hold that a man is justified by faith apart from works of law,"* writes Paul (Romans 3:28; Galatians 2:16). Salvation is a matter of God's free grace. We are justified by faith — not by works.

It was the Pharisees' proud rejection of grace — of help from above — that earned them Jesus' wrath. He could not help being sarcastic in His responses to them: *"Those who are well have no need of a physician, but those who are sick; I came not to call the righteous, but sinners"* (Mark 2:17; Matthew 9:12; Luke 5:31-2).

This emphasis on grace as it comes to us through God's redemptive acts in history might suggest an opposition between grace and law. When we adopt a redemptive historical stand-point, are we to dismiss any emphasis on God's law as "moralism"? If God constantly takes the initiative in the history of salvation, aren't our efforts to live by the law futile and unneeded?

To get this question into perspective, we must recognize that God's law is closely bound up with His covenant with His people, the covenant that ultimately goes back to the very beginning of human history. After the time of Abraham, the covenant involves a continuous line of people spoken of as the "descendants of Abraham." But the *law* came to that covenant community hundreds of years after Abraham, when the patriarchal family had swelled to form a nation. Was the covenant of grace made with Abraham replaced at Mount Sinai by a covenant of law?

Not at all. Paul explains: *"The law, which came four hundred and thirty years afterward, does not annul a covenant previously ratified by God, so as to make the promise void. For if the inheritance is by the law, it is no longer by promise; but God gave it to Abraham by a promise"* (Galatians 3:17-18). Thus, our keeping the law is *not* a condition for the fulfillment of the promise to Abraham. Christ was eventually to render perfect obedience on behalf of Abraham's descendants — including us.

We must learn to read the law within a covenant context. The law was not given as a piece of advice to mankind in general. God addressed the law specifically to His covenant people. They had gathered at Mount Sinai to pledge allegiance to their Lord and go through the ceremony that would make the covenant relationship official. It was during this series of events that God gave the Israelites the ten commandments (Exodus 20; Deuteronomy 5).

The law was part of the covenant agreement between the Lord and His people. Moses explained: *"And he declared to you his covenant, which he commanded you to perform, that is, the ten commandments; and he wrote them upon two tables of stone"* (Deuteronomy 4:13).

God's law is one channel through which His love for His people comes to expression. While it reminds them constantly of their sins, it also *gives life*. Therefore, it is a source of delight, as Psalm 119 emphasizes: *"Oh, how I love thy law! It is my meditation all the day"* (Verse 97). The law is also a source of blessing: *"Blessed are those whose way is blameless, who walk in the law of the Lord"* (Verse 1).

The Old Testament shows us in detail how that law can be applied to daily life. It gives numerous guidelines for human relationships and also provides regulations governing social matters in ancient Israel. Furthermore, it spells out ceremonial regulations for worship and offerings under the old dispensation of grace.

When we look at the law from the perspective of redemptive history, the confusion is quickly dispelled. Salvation comes to us from God and is not conditional upon our keeping the law. We keep the law to express our gratitude for the gift of salvation, and also because the law is a source of life and strength and renewal.

In this regard the law is definitely binding for New Testament believers, just as it was for the Old Testament saints. The only difference is that the Old Testament rituals and regulations that pointed ahead to Christ's redemptive work are now superfluous.

The key to keeping the law in a changing world is to learn a lesson from the mistakes of the Pharisees. The Pharisees lived by the letter of the law and ignored the law's *spirit*. We must begin with the spirit of the law and work out the guidelines required for our time and the situation in which we live.

This is what Jesus did in His time when He talked about the law. He complained that some people believed they were keeping the sixth commandment as long as they didn't kill anyone. They were mistaken, for they were substituting the letter of the law for the spirit: *"I say to you that every one who is angry with his brother shall be liable to judgment"* (Matthew 5:22).

He approached the seventh commandment in the same way. It is not enough to refrain from forbidden sexual relations, He insisted. *"Every one who looks at a woman lustfully has already committed adultery with her in his heart"* (Verse 28).

The provision about swearing was again a matter of the spirit of the law. *"You have heard that it was said to the men of old, 'You shall not swear falsely, but shall perform to the Lord what you have sworn.' But I say to you, Do not swear at all"* (Verses 33-4).

A redemptive historical approach to Scripture leaves plenty of room for an emphasis on the law — provided it is understood that our observance of the law is not the basis of our salvation. On this point Jesus left little room for confusion. He insisted that He had not come to set aside the law. On the contrary, He taught the same law of life that we find in the Old Testament.

We sometimes hear talk to the effect that Jesus taught a "law of love" that superseded all the Old Testament precepts and regulations:

> *You shall love the Lord your God with all your heart and with all your soul, and with all your mind. This is the great and first commandment. And a second is like it, You shall love your neighbor as yourself. On these two commandments depend all the law and the prophets* (Matthew 22:37-40).

This law is then hailed as a "higher law," a breakthrough to a new level of moral consciousness.

But this summary of the law, this statement of the law's spirit, is already to be found in the Old Testament. Joshua advised:

> *Take good care to observe the commandment and the law which Moses the servant of the Lord commanded you, to love the Lord your God, and to walk in all his ways, and to keep his commandments, and to cleave to him, and to serve him with all your heart and with all your soul* (Joshua 22:5).

Joshua, in turn, was pointing back to the words of Moses: "*You shall love the Lord your God with all your heart, and with all your soul, and with all your might*" (Deuteronomy 6:5). The second great commandment was also formulated by Moses: "*You shall love your neighbor as yourself*" (Leviticus 19:18).

Thus the New Testament emphasis on the spirit of the law is also present in the Old Testament. Samuel, confronted with Saul's efforts to please the Lord through sacrifices, declared: "*To obey is better than sacrifice, and to hearken than the fat of rams*" (I Samuel 15:22).

The law has a constant place within the framework of God's redemptive plan. Emphasis on the law is as timely today as in the days of the judges.

The Bible gives us directives for the various areas of life. We are to work out what is required of us in our time and situation, using as our model and general guideline the Bible's own way of applying the law of life in ancient times. Conditions change, and therefore we must be flexible. Yet, we should realize that any attempt to leave the law behind as a relic of an earlier stage in the history of salvation will lead to spiritual decay and ultimately death. The law gives life.

In our time, too, we must recognize that the law takes on its full meaning only within the covenant context. We tend to view Jesus as a teacher with moral lessons for the entire world, but His applications and explanations of the law were really intended for the *covenant community,* which is now open to people of all nations.

When we read the Sermon on the Mount, many of us love to lift out a text here or there and give it a universal meaning. For example, *"Blessed are the meek, for they shall inherit the earth"* (Matthew 5:5). Could this have something to do with Marxist visions of peasants and workers overthrowing the rich and powerful? *"Blessed are those who mourn, for they shall be comforted"* (Verse 4). Does this mean that the process of mourning leads to emotional health? Is Jesus teaching us psychology here?

When we read these beatitudes straight through, the covenant context is unmistakable. The beatitudes culminate in a promise and a reference to the Old Testament covenant people: *"Blessed are you when men revile you and persecute you and utter all kinds of evil against you falsely* on my account. *Rejoice and be glad, for your reward is great in heaven, for so men persecuted the prophets who were before you"* (Verses 11, 12).

This tells us whom Jesus had in mind when He spoke of the peacemakers, the pure in heart, those who are persecuted for righteousness' sake, and those who are merciful. He certainly didn't mean the secular humanists of our day with their liberal ideals.

When we look closely at the law, we see that genuine obedience is possible only for those who bow before God. Keeping the sabbath involves more than resting. Refraining from idolatry is possible only for those who worship the Creator of heaven and earth. The very language of the law presupposes a life of worship and service, a life within the covenant, a life in which the fruits of

Christ's redemptive work are allowed to grow.

We must not make the mistake of supposing that Christianity is a moral code *plus* a set of doctrines. That "moral code" only makes sense and leads to true blessing within a life lived out of a certain confession. Only those who confess the name of Jesus may call themselves Christians.

Unbelievers who refrain from murder and adultery and working on Sunday are not thereby living by the spirit of the law. All the same, they are benefiting from the law, for the life-giving law of God has benefits even for those who refuse to worship its author. Paul tells us that the Gentiles "*do by nature what the law requires*," even though they do not have the law (Romans 2:14). They do so not out of any love of God but because the law is a condition for the normal unfolding of life.

God's law is inescapable. But it has abiding, redemptive significance only within the circle of His covenant people. Love for that law may never be scorned as "moralism" or "legalism." We fall prey to those evils only when we lose sight of the spirit of the law and begin to believe that we can contribute to our own salvation and justification by obedience.

12

Prophecy and History

When we see how God uses history to reveal Himself and work out His redemptive purposes, we begin to wonder about our own history, about the centuries that have passed since the ascension of Christ and the writing of the New Testament. If the history of God's people is so significant, why do we have no inspired account of that history as it continues beyond the apostolic era? Why does the Bible end where it does? Doesn't the Bible have anything to say about our times and the events that lie ahead?

Redemptive history did not come to a close in Paul's time. There is still much that needs to be done and is being done. The final conquest of Satan and his forces still lies ahead. God is busy gathering His own all over the world.

Redemptive history goes on even though we have no inspired accounts and no divine commentary on it. God still works through men to achieve His purposes, just as He did in biblical times; but now we must learn to discern His hand for ourselves, using the Bible's redemptive history and divine commentary on it as our guide as we ponder the significance of events in our time.

This applies to both church history and the history of Christianity in general. Because God's Kingdom takes in much more than the church, the history of His people is more encompassing than the history of the church. God's people come together in the church as a community of faith and worship, but what they do beyond the framework of the church is also highly significant for God's purposes. All of world history is a stage on which God is working out His redemptive plan through the history and actions of His people.

But this is not to say that the history of Christianity is to be read as revelational history. In biblical times God revealed Himself in special ways and on numerous occasions. He used kings, priests, prophets, and other office-bearers to give His people some idea of who and what the coming Redeemer would be. The history of David's house, for example, must be read as revelational history.

Whereas David and other Old Testament saints pointed *forward* to a Christ who was to come, a Christ who could not yet be clearly seen, *we* must live our lives in such a way that we direct people's attention *back* to the New Testament Christ of whom the Old Testament prophesied. Once people recognize Him as King and Lord, they will learn to look ahead to the coming Christ who will reign in glory and renew the entire earth.

But even when we live our lives in a way that glorifies God and points to Christ, we are *not* serving as direct channels of divine revelation. Through our speech and conduct, we should make people think of *the Christ of the Scriptures*, the Christ who is already properly revealed to us in God's Word. We must not seek to add to the record of revelational history.

The Bible ends where it does because by that point God has told us all we need to know. We see that Jesus' promise of the Spirit, the "Comforter," was fulfilled at Pentecost. We also see that the question of the status of the Jews and the temple was settled decisively. (The destruction of Jerusalem and the temple, which we learn about from other sources, is alluded to often in the New Testament.) Once the Jews are stripped of any and all claims to special covenant privileges, the new age, which is repeatedly spoken of as the final age or "last hour," is upon us.

Still, one might ask, Doesn't the Bible prophesy about what lies ahead and tell us what will happen at the end of time? After all, Scripture is full of warnings about rough times ahead, times of persecution and conflict and apostasy. Can we look to biblical prophecy to give us at least an outline of the events to come?

This question is very difficult to answer. In fact, the application of biblical prophecy to the end of time is one of the most thorny of all interpretive problems. Hence all the confusion about such books as Daniel, Ezekiel and Revelation.

There are some Christians who maintain that many of the biblical prophecies, Old Testament and New, are finally being fulfilled in our own time. There are other Christians who disagree with them, arguing that those prophecies were already fulfilled centuries ago in biblical times.

The issue is not simply a matter of choosing between these two positions. What complicates things is that biblical prophecies sometimes have two — or even more — meanings. A prophecy that has already been fulfilled in some way may await further fulfillment.

To get this feature of biblical prophecy into focus, we should stop and consider the Bible's love of double meanings. I can think of no better illustration than a prophecy of Hosea quoted in the book of Matthew: "*Out of Egypt I called my son*" (Hosea 11:1). When we read this statement in its *Old Testament* context, its meaning seems obvious and far from mysterious: "*When Israel was a child, I loved him, and out of Egypt I called my son.*" Hosea seems to be making a statement about Israel's exodus from Egypt's house of bondage.

But Matthew calls this statement a prophecy and applies it to the time when Mary, Joseph and Jesus sought refuge from Herod in Egypt: *"This was to fulfil what the Lord had spoken by the prophet, 'Out of Egypt have I called my son'"* (2:15).

At first glance the Old Testament meaning seems too remote from Matthew's application for that application to be justifiable. Yet, this apparent remoteness is something we encounter regularly when we examine biblical prophecy.

One of the most famous prophecies in the book of Isaiah has the same kind of double meaning. Late in the history of Judah, King Ahaz finds himself in deep trouble. Syria and Israel are advancing on him. The prophet Isaiah comes to Ahaz with some words of reassurance and invites him to ask a sign of the Lord.

Ahaz refuses. But Isaiah offers him a sign anyway: "*Behold, a young woman shall conceive and bear a son and shall call his name Immanuel. . . . Before the child knows how to refuse the evil and choose the good, the land before whose two kings you are in dread will be deserted*" (Isaiah 7:14-16). This prophecy was presumably fulfilled in the time of Ahaz, although Scripture does not give us the details.

There must have been a young woman who gave birth to a child and gave him the beautiful name *Immanuel* (God with us). But our minds immediately leap ahead to Christ. And the New Testament does indeed apply this prophecy to Christ: "*All this took place to fulfil what the Lord had spoken by the prophet: 'Behold, a virgin shall conceive and bear a son, and his name shall be called Emmanuel'*" (Matthew 1:22-3). Again, the Old Testament prophecy has a double meaning, and the initial fulfillment is not the most important one.

We find the same pattern of multiple fulfillment in the prophecy of Ezekiel. Chapters 40 to 47 of Ezekiel give us a detailed account of a vision of a restored temple. Just before the record of this vision come some prophecies about the restoration of God's people, who were living in exile at the time. Did those prophecies only apply to the return to the promised land? Or were they also speaking of the eternal destiny of the people of God?

> *Now I will restore the fortunes of Jacob, and have mercy upon the whole house of Israel; and I will be jealous for my holy name. They shall forget their shame, and all the treachery they have practiced against me, when they dwell securely in their land with none to make them afraid, when I have brought them back from the peoples and gathered them from their enemies' lands, and through them have vindicated my holiness in the sight of many nations. Then they shall know that I am the Lord their God because I sent them into exile among the nations, and then gathered them into their own land (39:25-8).*

Up to this point it appears that Ezekiel is prophesying about the return from exile. But he goes on and says: "*I will leave none of them remaining among the nations any more; and I will not hide my face any more from them, when I pour out my Spirit upon the house of Israel"* (Verses 28-9). Here Ezekiel is clearly referring to the full and complete redemption foreshadowed by the return from exile, the redemption that will be realized when God's chosen ones are gathered in from all nations. Again, the prophecy seems to have a double meaning.

There is more we can learn from such a passage. It is not just a question of two unrelated or loosely connected meanings, as in a pun. From the prophet's perspective, those two redemptive events lie ahead and are not clearly distinct and separate. Indeed, God uses the one to reveal the other. To us they look distinct and separate, for one is in the past and the other is still mainly in the future. But Ezekiel tends to see them as one event.

Many Old Testament prophecies have this character: two distinct fulfillments that are not clearly separable when viewed from an Old Testament perspective.

God promised Abraham: *"I will make you exceedingly fruitful; and I will make nations of you, and kings shall come forth from you"* (Genesis 17:6, 16). We think of the kings of Israel, and especially of the house of David. Kings did indeed come forth from Abraham. But even more significant is the fact that the Redeemer, the long awaited Messiah-King, was born of Abraham's line. The greatest king of all "came forth" from Abraham!

David occupies a special place in the Old Testament because he makes us think of Christ. Psalm 78, which gives us an overview of Israel's history, presents that history as leading up to David:

He rejected the tent of Joseph,
he did not choose the tribe of Ephraim;
but he chose the tribe of Judah,
Mount Zion, which he loves.
He built his sanctuary like the high heavens,
like the earth, which he has founded for ever.
He chose David his servant,
and took him from the sheepfolds;
from tending the ewes that had young he brought him
to be the shepherd of Jacob his people,
of Israel his inheritance.

With upright heart he tended them,
and guided them with skilful hand (Verses 67-72).

When we read that David is the shepherd of God's people, we think immediately of Christ, the Good Shepherd. This psalm can also be read as speaking of Christ and pointing ahead to Him.

David is significant because he served as Israel's theocratic king and thereby reflected the glory of the king who was to come. The kingship always had a Messianic purpose in Israel; that's why apostasy on the part of Israel's king had to be punished so severely.

When we read the beautiful prayer for the king in Psalm 72, we recognize that the king is supposed to give the people what they will ultimately receive from their Redeemer-King. This psalm, too, has a profound double meaning.

Finally, Psalm 22 shows us something of how Old Testament prophecy should be read. This psalm grips us each time we read it because it opens with the haunting words Jesus spoke from the cross: "*My God, my God, why hast thou forsaken me?*" In this psalm David complains: "*They divide my garments among them, and for my raiment they cast lots*" (Verse 18). We think of the scene on Golgotha, where exactly that happened (Matthew 27: 35). Psalm 22 is to be read first of all as arising out of David's own experience, but it also speaks in an eloquent way of the suffering of Christ.

We must bear these double meanings in mind even in the *stories* about David. The friendship between Jonathan and David is one of the most celebrated friendships of all time, but there was more than friendship involved. Jonathan apparently had a clear sense of God's awesome purpose with David. That's why he not only befriended David but honored him. We read that Jonathan, the heir apparent to the throne, "*stripped himself of the robe that was upon him, and gave it to David, and his armor, and even his sword and his bow and his girdle*" (I Samuel 18:4). Jonathan clearly sensed David's destiny:

May the Lord be with you, as he has been with my father. If I am still alive, show me the loyal love of the Lord, that I may not die; and do not cut off your loyalty from my house for ever. When the Lord cuts off every one of the enemies of David from the face of the earth, let not the name of Jonathan be cut off from the house of David. And may the Lord take vengeance upon David's enemies (20:13-16).

The Lord's cause is here identified with David's cause. At their last meeting, Jonathan again honors David: "*You shall be king over Israel*" (23:17). As Jonathan bows before David, we are reminded that we must bow before the greatest member of David's house and revere Him just as Jonathan revered his best friend.

Similar honors came to David from Abigail, the wife of Nabal, who later became his own wife:

The Lord will certainly make my lord a sure house, because my lord is fighting the battles of the Lord; and evil shall not be found in you so long as you live. If men rise up to pursue you and to seek your life, the life of my lord shall be bound in the bundle of the living in the care of the Lord your God; and the lives of your enemies he shall sling out as from the hollow of a sling (25:28-9).

This, too, is prophecy with a double meaning.

The many prophecies about the "day of the Lord" likewise have a double meaning. They speak to us of both judgment and deliverance. Joel prophesies:

Blow the trumpet in Zion;
sound the alarm on my holy mountain!
Let all the inhabitants of the land tremble,
for the day of the Lord is coming, it is near,
a day of darkness and gloom,
a day of clouds and thick darkness! (2:1-2).

He paints a gloomy picture indeed: "*For the day of the Lord is great and very terrible; who can endure it?*" (Verse 11). But in the very same chapter, Joel gives us glorious prophecies of deliverance, culminating in the stirring words that Peter also chose to quote in his Pentecost sermon:

> *And it shall come to pass afterward,*
> *that I will pour out my spirit on all flesh;*
> *your sons and your daughters shall prophesy,*
> *your old men shall dream dreams,*
> *and your young men shall see visions* (Verse 28).

Zephaniah says of the day of the Lord: "*The Lord has prepared a sacrifice and consecrated his guests*" (1:7).

Zechariah also speaks of "that day" in optimistic terms: "*Behold, a day of the Lord is coming, when the spoil taken from you will be divided in the midst of you*" (14:1).

In the New Testament, the "day of the Lord" is identified as the day of Christ's return. Paul writes: "*The day of the Lord will come like a thief in the night. When people say, 'There is peace and security,' then sudden destruction will come upon them as travail comes upon a woman with child, and there will be no escape*" (I Thessalonians 5:2-3). But that day of destruction and judgment is a day of deliverance for believers: "*You are not in darkness, brethren, for that day to surprise you like a thief*" (Verse 4).

The Old Testament prophets tended to see the incarnation and Christ's final coming in glory as one event, one "day of the Lord." From our New Testament perspective, however, we now see that the prophecies about the "day of the Lord" have more than one fulfillment. History has seen more than one "day of the Lord" involving judgment as the dominant note. (Think of the destruction of Jerusalem and the temple in A.D. 70.) Today we await the final day of the Lord, which will bring judgment on the earth as well as complete renewal after Christ's return in majesty.

It is clear, then, that biblical prophecies that have already been fulfilled may await further fulfillment, especially those in which two related events are run together.

Daniel 11, which is a difficult passage, exemplifies this pattern. Most interpreters are agreed that this chapter speaks of the persecution of the Jews under the Syrian king Antiochus Epiphanes in the third century B.C. But the parallel between

Daniel's prophecy and the career of this king is not complete.

It appears that the prophecy is also meant as a commentary on the deeds of some future antichrist. However, the shift from one set of circumstances to the other is not clear. This suggests the possibility that much of what is described in Daniel 11 will one day be repeated. In other words, Daniel 11 may be a prophecy with a double fulfillment.

We find the same kind of shift and double meaning in Mark 13, where Jesus is talking about what lies ahead for Jerusalem. He begins His remarks when one of His disciples points to the temple. Jesus talks about the misery and judgment in store for the great city and the worship community of the temple because of its refusal to accept the Messiah. Then He draws his disciples' attention to some signs of the times.

Jesus goes on, however, to make some statements about a time beyond the days of Jerusalem's destruction:

The stars will be falling from heaven, and the powers in the heavens will be shaken. And then they will see the Son of man coming in clouds with great power and glory. And then he will send out the angels, and gather his elect from the four winds, from the ends of the earth to the ends of heaven (Mark 13:25-7).

Here Jesus is talking about His return in glory. The close connection in this passage between the destruction of Jerusalem and Christ's return in glory suggests that before His return there will be certain events paralleling Jerusalem's destruction.

It appears that the question of whether the Bible's prophecies apply to our time cannot be answered with a simple yes or no. On the one hand, biblical prophecy deals mainly with the biblical era, which includes the coming of the Messiah, His ascension to glory, and the outpouring of the Spirit. On the other hand, the Bible uses prophecies about the coming of the Messiah and various judgments during the biblical era to point to other events further in the future, events that are still ahead of us. It does not describe those events in any detail, but it does reveal what is at issue: the age-old struggle between the seed of the woman and the seed of the serpent.

13

The Day of Salvation and the Last Things

When Christians look for light on the "last things," they usually open the book of Revelation, a book that is notoriously difficult to understand and interpret. Despite the confusion and potential dangers, however, we must proceed on the assumption that this often puzzling book was included in the Bible for our instruction and edification. Therefore we should do our best to fathom its meaning, steering clear of the danger of unfounded speculation about the future.

As we read Revelation, we should keep the double-fulfillment character of biblical prophecy in mind. This book speaks first of all to the churches of the apostolic era and describes some of the early persecution, but it is also intended to tell us something about the "last things," especially in the final chapters.

Before we turn to the book of Revelation, however, we should consider the question of how God's covenant with the Jews is transformed in the post-ascension, post-Pentecost era. The answer, in brief, is that the covenant is opened up to people of all tribes and tongues, which the Pentecost event so beautifully symbolizes with its tongues of fire and its Babel of languages, all expressing the same gospel message.

The good news about Jesus Christ now goes out to all men and nations. In Old Testament times, God had "*allowed all the nations to walk in their own ways,*" as Paul put it (Acts 14:16). But it was always His intention to spread the light of His Word and His glory over the nations, the Gentiles. The four gospels emphasize this point, echoing the Old Testament.

Aged Simeon, holding the baby Jesus in his arms, sings: "*Mine eyes have seen thy salvation which thou hast prepared in the presence of all peoples, a light for revelation to the Gentiles*" (Luke 2:30-2). Those Gentiles had long been left to themselves to walk in their own ways, far removed from the light.

But all this changed with the coming of the Messiah. Hence Zechariah could sing joyfully about the salvation that would now come to "*those who sit in darkness and in the shadow of death*" (Luke 1:79). Matthew sang the same song: "*The people who sat in darkness have seen a great light*" (4:16). He was echoing the song of Isaiah:

> *Behold my servant, whom I uphold,*
> *my chosen, in whom my soul delights;*
> *I have put my Spirit upon him,*
> *he will bring forth justice to the nations.*
> *He will not fail or be discouraged*
> *till he has established justice in the earth;*
> *and the coastlands wait for his law* (Isaiah 42:1, 4).

The new age, then, is the age of the Gentiles, of the nations. In the Old Testament period, Israel's people were God's special possession (Exodus 19:5). Membership in the covenant was only possible for outsiders through membership in Israel as a nation. (Think of Rahab and Ruth.) It was in Israel's midst that God chose to dwell, and all Israel was blessed with His presence.

The sign of that presence was the ark of the covenant, which was kept in the tabernacle and later in the temple. Once, when the ark was lost, a discerning believer saw immediately what the loss meant. Dying as she gave birth, the wife of Phinehas called her baby *Ichabod* — "*The glory has departed from Israel*" (I Samuel 4:21-2).

But it was God's intention that His glory remain in the midst of

Israel and ultimately fill the earth. That's why the covenant had to be opened to people of all nations, which meant that membership in a particular nation would no longer be a condition for membership in the covenant. The broadening of the covenant was a step toward the time when God's presence and glory would no longer be localized. One day, declared the prophet Habakkuk, *"the earth will be filled with the knowledge of the glory of the Lord, as the waters cover the sea"* (Habakkuk 2:14). Then the temple and the ark will no longer be needed as vehicles of God's presence, for the Immanuel promise ("God with us") will be fully realized.

The period after Pentecost and Christ's ascension is the time in which the nations are liberated, set free, led out of darkness into Christ's marvelous light. Isaiah foresaw it:

The Lord has bared his holy arm
before the eyes of all the nations;
and all the ends of the earth shall see
the salvation of our God (Isaiah 52:10).

Paul and the other apostles did not bring the gospel to the Gentiles because the Jews refused to listen: *"to the Jew first,"* said Paul, *"and* also *to the Greek"* (Romans 1:16). The fact is that many of the Jews did listen and believe. The Jews were to hear the gospel first — but not exclusively.

In Antioch (Pisidia), Paul and Barnabas explained to the Jews:

It was necessary that the word of God should be spoken first to you. Since you thrust it from you, and judge yourselves unworthy of eternal life, behold, we turn to the Gentiles. For so the Lord has commanded us, saying, "I have set you to be a light for the Gentiles, that you may bring salvation to the uttermost parts of the earth (Acts 13:46-7; Isaiah 49:6).

Jesus Himself had made it clear long before that the gospel call was to go out to all the nations:

Go therefore and make disciples of all nations, baptizing them in the name of the Father and of the Son and of the Holy Spirit,

teaching them to observe all that I have commanded you
(Matthew 28:19-20).

The question of the nations or the Gentiles must not be forgotten as we read Revelation and ponder the meaning of the binding of Satan:

*Then I saw an angel coming down from heaven, holding in his
hand the key of the bottomless pit and a great chain. And he
seized the dragon, that ancient serpent, who is the Devil and
Satan, and bound him for a thousand years, and threw him into
the pit, and shut it and sealed it over him, that he should deceive
the nations no more, till the thousand years were ended. After
that he must be loosed for a little while* (Revelation 20:1-3).

This vision of a thousand-year period, which we usually take to be the period between Christ's ascension and the "last things," presents Satan as restricted in his activities. More specifically, we are told that he can "*deceive the nations no more.*" No longer do the nations languish in darkness. Later in this chapter we read that he is to be let loose again for a while. Then comes the end — the final triumph of Christ.

Revelation 20 is followed immediately by the beautiful vision of the new heaven and the new earth. John sees the new Jerusalem, and he hears the promise that God will wipe away every tear (Revelation 21:2-4).

The period between Christ's ascension and the last things is the time of the Gentiles. Jesus explains that Jerusalem "*will be trodden down by the Gentiles, until the times of the Gentiles are fulfilled*" (Luke 21:24). At the very end we see a new, restored Jerusalem in which the redemptive promises made to both Jews and Gentiles are fulfilled, a new Jerusalem on a new earth under a new heaven.

The Bible does have something to say, then, about the redemptive history yet to come. We are living in a time when the Gentiles are free from their bondage to sin and Satan. No longer does God pronounce the ban on entire nations like the Amalekites and the people of Sodom and Gomorrah. There is still much wickedness on the earth, but in all the nations (we see this fulfilled especially in our own day) God is busy gathering His church.

The Bible gives us a characterization of the age in which we live. It is a time of great opportunity: "*Behold, now is the acceptable time; behold, now is the day of salvation*" (II Corinthians 6:2). God continues to postpone judgment as He lets His Word go out to the four corners of the earth.

The conclusion of the book of Acts strikes the note that characterizes our time. Satan has been bound and can deceive the nations no more. We are given a picture of Paul living in Rome, the heart of the civilization of his day, "*preaching the kingdom of God and teaching about the Lord Jesus Christ quite openly and unhindered*" (28:31).

Paul was living by the command of His master: "*We must work the works of him who sent me, while it is day; night comes, when no one can work*" (John 9:4). That night has not yet fallen. Late in the twentieth century, we still enjoy the privilege of living during the "day of salvation."

14

The Language of Scripture

My purpose in writing was to help believers understand the Bible better as they read it. My special aim was to open people's eyes to the historical dimension present in so many of the stories and prophecies contained in the Bible. The history recorded in Scripture is *our* history, for we, too, are children of Abraham and heirs of the glorious promise he received.

It was not my intention to deal explicity with hermeneutics and the principles of exegesis. Still, in conclusion I would like to plead for an open approach to the language of Scripture, an approach not prejudiced by assumptions and presuppositions foreign to Scripture.

It seems to me that interpreters of the Bible often go wrong because of a false preoccupation with "translation" — the translation of biblical terms and concepts into concepts that fit the thinking of modern man in the age of nuclear weapons and the computer. The twentieth century debate about "demythologizing" illustrates what I am getting at.

The point that ought to be stressed instead is that the Bible's redemptive concepts, including many of those dealt with in the foregoing chapters, have a normative status for believers; that is to say, they are part of the authoritative message the Bible proclaims to us. Therefore, we need not and should not "translate" them into the language and thought patterns of our time.

If we are willing to bow in obedience before the Bible's good news that Jesus is the Redeemer promised in the Old Testament, we should not reject the language in which this good news comes to us by declaring it unfit for our time. We cannot separate the Bible's message completely from the language in which that message is phrased. It is not enough to say that God's Word comes to us *in* the Bible; we must go further and affirm that the Bible *is* God's Word.

If we are willing to join in this age-old confession about the Bible's divine origin and authority, we must let our thinking and language be shaped by the basic biblical concepts in which the message of redemption through Jesus Christ comes to us. Those concepts cannot be set out and explained within the framework of reference and meaning provided by any one scientific discipline — not even history. In this sense it is certainly true that the Bible is not a textbook. The Bible is *sui generis* — a book unlike any other — for it speaks to man from a perspective that transcends his own experience, a perspective anchored in eternity.

We must be willing to live with a degree of imprecision in our understanding of the Bible. The lack of precision in biblical language and concepts may be irksome to some scholars who make their living studying the Bible, but the Bible was not written to measure up to the standards of accuracy, detail and completeness embraced by scholars in our age — or any age, for that matter.

It seems to me that we ought to approach the Bible in something of the same frame of mind that we bring to a literary work. The Bible's language is concrete, suggestive and colorful, but it is rarely abstract, precise and scientific. It leaves us with more impressions than definitions.

Those impressions, engraved in our hearts and minds through the mediation of God's Spirit, are a source of rich blessing for us, just as they were for those Old Testament believers who understood comparatively little of what the promise of redemption meant. When we open our minds and hearts fully to scriptural language and seek to be instructed without imposing our ideas and categories on the Bible, we, too, can say:

> *How sweet are thy words to my taste,*
> *sweeter than honey to my mouth!*
> *Through thy precepts I get understanding;*
> *therefore I hate every false way.*
> *Thy word is a lamp to my feet*
> *and a light to my path* (Psalm 119:103-5).

Subject Index

Index of Scripture References

WITHDRAWN